Programs for Older Adults

Morris A. Okun, *Editor*

D1301090

NEW DIRECTIONS FOR CONTINUING EDUCATION

ALAN B. KNOX, *Editor-in-Chief*

Number 14, June 1982

Paperback sourcebooks in
The Jossey-Bass Higher Education Series

Jossey-Bass Inc., Publishers
San Francisco • Washington • London

Programs for Older Adults
Number 14, June 1982
    Morris A. Okun, *Editor*

New Directions for Continuing Education Series
Alan B. Knox, *Editor-in-Chief*

Copyright © 1982 by Jossey-Bass Inc., Publishers
                and
            Jossey-Bass Limited

Copyright under International, Pan American, and Universal
Copyright Conventions. All rights reserved. No part of
this issue may be reproduced in any form — except for brief
quotation (not to exceed 500 words) in a review or professional
work — without permission in writing from the publishers.

New Directions for Continuing Education (publication number
USPS 493-930) quarterly by Jossey-Bass Inc., Publishers.
Second-class postage rates paid at San Francisco, California,
and at additional mailing offices.

Correspondence:
Subscriptions, single-issue orders, change of address notices,
undelivered copies, and other correspondence should be sent to
New Directions Subscriptions, Jossey-Bass Inc., Publishers,
433 California Street, San Francisco, California 94104.

Editorial correspondence should be sent to the Editor-in-Chief,
Alan B. Knox, Teacher Education Building, Room 264,
University of Wisconsin, 225 North Mills Street, Madison,
Wisconsin 53706.

Saint Mary's University Library
197029

Library of Congress Catalogue Card Number LC 81-48475
International Standard Serial Number ISSN 0195-2242
International Standard Book Number ISBN 87589-888-2

Cover art by Willi Baum
Manufactured in the United States of America

Ordering Information

The paperback sourcebooks listed below are published quarterly and can be ordered either by subscription or as single copies.

Subscriptions cost $35.00 per year for institutions, agencies, and libraries. Individuals can subscribe at the special rate of $21.00 per year *if payment is by personal check.* (Note that the full rate of $35.00 applies if payment is by institutional check, even if the subscription is designated for an individual.) Standing orders are accepted.

Single copies are available at $7.95 when payment accompanies order, and *all single-copy orders under $25.00 must include payment.* (California, Washington, D.C., New Jersey, and New York residents please include appropriate sales tax.) For billed orders, cost per copy is $7.95 plus postage and handling. (Prices subject to change without notice.)

To ensure correct and prompt delivery, all orders must give either the *name of an individual* or an *official purchase order number.* Please submit your order as follows:

Subscriptions: specify series and subscription year.
Single Copies: specify sourcebook code and issue number (such as, CE8).

Mail orders for United States and Possessions, Latin America, Canada, Japan, Australia, and New Zealand to:
Jossey-Bass Inc., Publishers
433 California Street
San Francisco, California 94104

Mail orders for all other parts of the world to:
Jossey-Bass Limited
28 Banner Street
London EC1Y 8QE

New Directions for Continuing Education Series
Alan B. Knox, *Editor-in-Chief*

Contents

Editor's Notes

Continuing education programs have, to a large extent, ignored the interests and concerns of those in the latter third of life. Individuals born in the early portion of the twentieth century tend to have less formal education than those born later. Presumably, they need more education to catch up. However, there is a sharp decline in participation beyond age fifty-five, and older adults with less formal education are less likely than their more formally educated peers to participate in programs. Clearly, an aging-education paradox exists; older adults represent a hard-to-reach group.

However, there has been considerable growth in programs for older adults over the last thirty years. Due to demographic shifts and social and technological changes, lifelong education is projected to increase in the immediate future. The purpose of this sourcebook is to explore life span developmental concepts and geropsychological research findings, along with current and potential program development responses by continuing educators.

How can concepts about life span development contribute to programming? What are the implications of laboratory findings on learning and memory for instruction? The perspective emerging from developmental theorizing and research is largely positive; age per se accounts for little of the variation in cognitive performance, and older adults exhibit plasticity in their cognitive functioning. Older adults make use of their potential for learning both in and out of educational settings. In response to their needs, programs have been initiated by religious institutions, pre- and postsecondary educational institutions, senior citizen centers, and so on. The illustrations of some of these efforts contained in this sourcebook provide descriptions that can be useful to continuing educators.

The first section of this sourcebook reviews the literature to provide a context for practitioners. In Chapters One and Two, Willis and Hulicka and Gounard summarize current ideas about life span development and research on age differences in learning and memory. The chapter by Waskel provides an overview of the state of the art of programs for older adults. She raises several questions about whether programmers are achieving their goals.

The second section contains three chapters that describe existing programs for older adults. Examples are drawn from the leading providers, such as religious institutions (Maves), schools (Price), and community colleges (Demko). Principles from these programs can be adopted by programmers working in similar settings. A fourth chapter by Levenson describes the complexity of the relationships between educational providers and governmental agencies responsible for planning and coordination. He highlights the need for an integrated and cooperative venture among providers and various community agencies in the public and private sectors.

The concluding section consists of two chapters that explore some of the emerging issues that are important for those seeking to enhance the quality of older adult education. Specific recommendations are provided to facilitate participation and learning.

A final word on the terms *older adults* and *cohorts:* In the context of this sourcebook, older adults are individuals at least fifty-five years old. This criterion, although somewhat arbitrary, is consistent with current discussions of the "young old" (fifty-five through seventy) and the "old old" (seventy-one years and older) and of fifty-seven through sixty-five as the period during which the late-adult transition occurs.

In adult developmental psychology, researchers have become acutely aware that differences in performance between age groups measured at the same point in time may be due to intergenerational differences, as opposed to aging effects. Thus, the term *cohort* has been introduced to refer to a group of individuals born in close temporal proximity. For example, we refer to individuals born immediately after World War II as the "baby boom" cohort.

Morris A. Okun
Editor

Morris A. Okun received his doctoral training in educational psychology and postdoctoral training in aging from The Pennsylvania State University and Duke University, respectively. He is currently associate professor of higher and adult education at Arizona State University. He is presently collaborating on a meta-analysis of research on life satisfaction in adulthood and a book on literacy and the community college.

*The individual continues to develop across the total life course
and thus educational opportunities must be provided
to facilitate and optimize the development of older adults.*

Concepts from Life Span Developmental Psychology: Implications for Programming

Sherry L. Willis

During the past two decades, increasing attention has been given to a life span orientation within both developmental psychology and education. In the field of education, a life span perspective has been discussed under rubrics such as lifelong learning, recurrent education, nontraditional education, and continuing education. While never a dominant approach, the life span perspective has had its proponents throughout the history of psychology (see Baltes, 1979). It may be of particular interest to educators that Sidney Pressey, known for his pioneering work on teaching machines, coauthored one of the earliest life span texts in American psychology (Pressey, Janney, and Kuhlen, 1939). Even slightly earlier was E. L. Thorndike's (1928) major work on adult learning.

The recent revival of interest in a life span approach can be linked to a number of contemporaneous events. First, there is the shift in the age structure of Western industrialized societies. As the average life expectancy has increased in this century, the number of persons over sixty-five years in the United States has doubled from 1950 to 1980. Second, during the last three decades findings from a number of longitudinal studies focusing on the adult years have been reported. These longitudinal studies include both research

M. Okun (Ed.). *New Directions for Continuing Education: Programs for Older Adults*, no. 14.
San Francisco: Jossey-Bass, June 1982.

specifically on development across the adult years (Palmore, 1974) and also follow-up studies on aging participants from several child-growth studies (Bayley, 1968). These longitudinal studies have contributed significantly to our understanding of development and change during adulthood. Thus, both sociocultural trends and a more comprehensive knowledge base regarding adult development have added to the renewed interest in a life span approach to development and education.

In this chapter, we will begin by discussing several critical features of a life span developmental perspective. Then, the issue of the modifiability of cognitive functioning in later adulthood will be explored. Finally, implications of a life span perspective for educational research and practice will be considered.

Critical Features of a Life Span Developmental Orientation

Life span developmental psychology is best characterized as a perspective or an approach to the study of development, rather than as a specific theory or model of development. The life span perspective is not linked to a specific area of development (for example, cognition) or age period (adulthood), nor is it necessarily aligned with one particular theoretical persuasion (for example, cognitive developmental or behavioral). Rather, a life span perspective seeks to understand the developing individual across the entire life course within a changing sociocultural context. A life span perspective seeks to define the pattern or sequences of developmental change across the life course. It examines the interrelationships among developmental periods. One could, for example, study changes in achievement motivation from childhood through adulthood. The interrelationship between achievement motivation in childhood and patterns of achievement in adulthood could be examined. In addition, the impact of cultural change on achievement motivation in different generations (cohorts) can be considered. Functioning in later adulthood reflects cumulative developmental change and experiences across the life course. Thus, an understanding of patterns and interrelationships in life span development would appear particularly important to those providing educational programs for older adults.

A life span perspective assumes that (1) significant developmental change occurs across the total life course (Baltes and Willis, 1979a, 1979b; Brim and Kagan, 1980); (2) developmental change is both quantitative (change in level, rate, degree) and qualitative (change in nature, type) (Labouvie-Vief, 1977); and (3) developmental change across the life course is multidirectional. It is critical that continuing educators take into account multidirectional patterns of development in adulthood in developing appropriate instructional strategies. For example, the educator may need to adapt the pacing of instruction in consideration of behavioral slowing with age. However, the educator should not infer a necessary decline or deficit in verbal ability although the older adult may write or speak more slowly.

Increasing Individual Differences. A major theme focuses on the increasing range of differences between individuals across the life span (Baltes and Willis, 1979a). In many areas of physical, cognitive, and social development, the range of variability or differences between individuals of the same chronological age is greater in adulthood than in childhood. For example, most normal children achieve developmental milestones such as walking, talking, and entering school within a relatively restricted age range; children do not differ greatly in the age at which these tasks are accomplished. However, adults vary considerably in the chronological age associated with such events as marriage, birth of first child, graying of hair, and menopause. Moreover, there appear to be far fewer developmental events in adulthood that could be considered universal for all or most adults. Only a portion of the adult population encounters even such so-called normative events as marriage and parenting.

The increase in the degree of variability among individuals in adulthood has several implications for adult development and education. First, it becomes more difficult to define developmental stages or norms that can be used to describe most adults. Some psychologists seriously question whether such adult stages of development can be identified at all. Moreover, even if such stages or developmental tasks can be defined, the age at which people experience a stage is much more variable. Chronological age, then, becomes a less useful index of development in adulthood. Intellectual abilities or levels of verbal ability, for example, appear to be more closely related to educational level or sociocultural experience than with chronological age per se. Within the educational context, instructional grouping by chronological age (as practiced with children) may be a less efficient instructional procedure than grouping by initial ability level, relevant life experiences, or adult interests.

It is likely that the narrow age band within which individual differences occur in childhood is associated with the greater isomorphy between biological and behavioral development in the early years. The rate and sequence of physiological development imposes a timetable on many aspects of behavior development in childhood. In addition, age-graded cultural institutions (ages for compulsory schooling, driver's license, and so on) may promote a close alignment between chronological age and certain developmental events in childhood (Riley, 1977). In contrast, once biological maturity has been achieved, behavioral development is less closely linked to biologically determined processes until, perhaps, very old age. Environmental and experiential factors come to play a far more pervasive role in adult development. Such environmental factors become not only more influential, but also more diverse in adulthood. This diversity of experiences contributes to the increasing individual differences in adulthood. Environmental influences may range from specific experiences unique to a given individual (for example, great wealth, death of parent in childhood) to broad-scale, historically significant events, such as war or depression, which affect an entire generation. This focus on environmental influences in adulthood leads to consideration of a third critical issue in a life span perspective.

Age Change Versus Sociocultural Change. Another major theme is that individuals experience dramatic cultural change throughout life. Cultural change becomes more extensive and significant as the individual grows older and the impact of change becomes cumulative. The term *cohort* refers to individuals who were born within a given time period and thus whose development may have been influenced by social and cultural events occurring during that period in history. Cohorts experience different environmental events and cultural change. For example, individuals born in 1917 (whose current age is sixty-five) were preschool children during World War I, experienced the Depression during adolescence, and were involved in World War II as young adults. In contrast, individuals born in 1947 (now thirty-five years old) were part of the postwar baby boom and grew up in a period of postwar affluence and rapid technological change. Whereas a high school education seemed a lofty goal for many of today's sixty-five-year-olds, current thirty-five-year-olds were often expected to complete college.

Different generations (cohorts) not only experience very different types of cultural change, but also experience them at different periods of development. War or depression may have quite different effects if experienced as a child rather than an adult. Given such diverse life experiences for various cohorts, we may expect that current thirty-five-year-olds will be quite different as sixty-five-year-olds in the year 2012 than today's sixty-five-year-olds. The adult educator or researcher studying only one such cohort of sixty-five-year-olds will develop a much different view of aging than the educator or researcher who studies and compares several cohorts of sixty-five-year-olds. It is important that educators and researchers differentiate between cohort differences and normative age changes — developmental changes that are common to and apply to adults of all cohorts. To differentiate cohort effects (unique to a particular cohort) from normative age change (common across cohorts), it is necessary to study several cohorts of adults at the same series of chronological ages. Relatively few such cohort-sequential studies have been conducted. However, one such study examining cohort differences versus age changes in adult intelligence is of particular interest with regard to adult educational endeavors. Schaie and Parham (1977) contrasted seven-year age changes with seven-year cohort differences. Results suggested that until the sixties there are no age changes on power tests but substantial cohort differences prevail. On the other hand, for highly speeded tests, cohort differences are relatively unimportant, while decremental age changes are detected in the forties. In terms of significant age changes (decline) in mental abilities such as reasoning and vocabulary, they were not found until the late sixties or early seventies. Thus, throughout much of adulthood cohort differences in intellectual functioning maybe of greater importance to adult educators than age changes per se.

Such cohort effects can impact different aspects of educatonal programming for the older adult. For example, interviews with older cohorts suggests that there may be cohort differences in learning strategies that are associated with early schooling. Earlier cohorts' schooling may have emphasized rote memorization in contrast to emphasis on principles, rules, and discovery approaches advocated today in education for the young. Second, there appear to be cohort differences in subject matter taught in elementary and secondary grades. Courses in algebra, geometry, psychology, and so on, are relatively recent innovations in secondary education. Third, educational testing and assessment procedures have changed through the years. Extensive use of standardized achievement and intelligence tests common in elementary and secondary education today were less common prior to World War II.

Modifiability of Intellectual Functioning
in Later Adulthood

The necessity of a lifelong approach to learning and education should be evident. However, until quite recently adult educational efforts in later adulthood were hampered by the myth of intellectual decline. It was assumed that learning ability was seriously limited in old age and that intellectual functioning showed a steep and pervasive decline. Stereotypic notions suggested that "you can't teach an old dog new tricks" or that adults become "set in their ways." This focus on decrement in adulthood has often been accompanied by the assumption that such cognitive change was irreversible. These assumptions have been largely based on correlations between physical changes in later adulthood and intellectual performance. While some decrement does occur, at least in very old age, and may be partially due to physical causes, assumptions regarding the pervasiveness of such decline and its irreversibility need to be re-examined. In contrast to the numerous cognitive intervention programs established for children, relatively few broad-based intervention programs have been conducted to modify and optimize intellectual functioning in old age. Therefore, we have limited knowledge of the extent to which areas of adult development could be modified and optimized.

Recall that longitudinal research, such as that by Schiae and Parham

(1977), suggests that intellectual functioning with regard to many mental abilities is relatively stable throughout much of adulthood with significant decline occurring in healthy older adults only in the sixties. In contrast, environmental and experiential factors, such as those associated with cohort effects, have been shown to impact intellectual functioning, even in young and middle adulthood. The lower level of performance noted for today's older adult when compared with today's young adult may then be less a function of intellectual decline with age, but rather a function of environmental differences experienced by the two cohorts in adulthood. To what extent can intellectual performance in later life be modified, then, through experiential and educational interventions? Some intellectual traits set down early in life may be relatively difficult to change. Other behaviors may be much more amenable to change at later stages in life. For firm conclusions to be reached, each cognitive ability of interest must be studied using several different training techniques.

A small but growing literature has reported successful modification of apparent low levels of performance in later adulthood for a variety of cognitive tasks (Hornblum and Overton, 1976; Willis, Blieszner, and Baltes, 1981). Moreover, in some studies such improvement in cognitive performance has been shown to be maintained up to six months following intervention and to generalize to related ability tasks. Such intervention programs have frequently been relatively brief (lasting only a few sessions) and less intensive than many cognitive intervention programs for young children. It has been suggested then that older adults may not be learning the cognitive skills de novo (as children do), but rather that such intervention programs activate cognitive skills and abilities already within the older adults' repertoire, but not spontaneously shown in their intellectual performance.

Significant improvement as a result of practice was shown in a recent study (Hofland, Willis, and Baltes, 1981). Older adults were asked to practice two types of problem-solving tasks on eight different occasions. These adults were given no feedback regarding the correctness of their answers or whether they were improving across sessions. For both of the problem-solving tasks, mean performance improved approximately 10 percent. Because the older adults were given no instruction on strategies for solving the tasks, such improvement reflects the adults' ability to activate and use cognitive skills already within their repertoire.

In addition, lower levels of intellectual performance have been associated with a variety of noncognitive factors (for example, lack of test sophistication, anxiety, slow behavioral responding, increased cautiousness). While such noncognitive factors are not intrinsic to intellectual abilities per se, they may affect intellectual performance. Intervention programs focusing on these factors have also been successful (Birkhill and Schaie, 1975; Hofland, Willis, and Baltes, 1981).

Implications of a Life Span Perspective
for Educational Practice

Expanding the Concept and Goals of Education. A life span approach suggests that individual development must be studied in the context of sociocultural change. Traditionally, education has tended to define goals in terms of either normative or differential views of individual development. Emphasis on normative patterns of development has led education to focus on developmental tasks. In contrast, emphasis on individual differences has resulted in a concern for differentiation and individualization of educational objectives. A life span perspective would consider both normative and differential developmental patterns in the context of social change, and thus would suggest three sources of educational goals. These are normative developmental tasks, individual variability, and sociocultural change. Individualization of educational goal setting becomes increasingly important with the wider range of individual differences in development during adulthood. Moreover, educational goals must be sensitive and adaptive to social change. This suggests not only that education must be responsive to social change but also that education can be involved in directing the nature of such change. It is evident that education can remediate for obsolescence due to social change and can also provide individuals with generic skills for coping, adapting to, and optimizing their development in relation to future change.

Instructional Methodology. Individual variability in almost every type of intellectual capacity increases across the life span. The greater range of individual differences in adulthood should be of primary concern to the educator. Extreme individual differences in an educational population usually require an individualized instructional approach. Such an individualized orientation would seem imperative in adult instruction. Variability in noncognitive factors related to learning, as well as in cognitive ability and motivation, must be considered in designing instructional approaches for the adult learner. Studies investigating the relationship between learner aptitudes and limitations and instructional approaches would appear particularly relevant in mapping out appropriate instructional strategies for the older adult learner.

The role of the instructor for participants across the life span appears to change from director of learning to that of a facilitator or resource person. Whereas society and the educator direct the education of the young, the content and method of learning in adulthood are largely determined by the learner. Developmental changes in the learner across the life span suggest the need for qualitatively different types of teacher training for educators working with different age groups. The techniques of the high school or even college instructor may be inappropriate in teaching middle-aged or older persons. Teacher training institutions must be involved in providing information concerning adult development and learning to continuing educators. Principles applying to the older adult learner may equally apply to the teacher's own continued updating and learning endeavors.

In summary, a lifelong approach to learning broadens the concepts of education beyond the traditional youth-oriented preparation for adulthood. Education serves preventive, facilitative, remedial, and preparatory functions. The focus of educational intervention extends beyond the acquisition of academic and vocational skills to enable the individual to master developmental tasks associated with each period in the life span. Thus, a lifelong view of education suggests the need for a reallocation of educational opportunity across the life span. The individual continues to develop across the total life course, and thus educational opportunities must be provided to facilitate and optimize the development of older adults.

References

Baltes, P. B. "Life Span Developmental Psychology: Observations on History and Theory." In P. B. Baltes and O. G. Brim, Jr. (Eds.), *Life Span Development and Behavior* (Vol. 2). New York: Academic Press, 1979.

Baltes, P. B., and Willis, S. L. "The Critical Importance of Appropriate Methodology in the Study of Aging: The Sample Case of Psychometric Intelligence." In F. Hoffmeister and C. Muller (Eds.), *Brain Function in Old Age.* Heidelberg, Germany: Springer, 1979a.

Baltes, P. B., and Willis, S. L. "Life Span Developmental Psychology, Cognitive Functioning, and Social Policy." In M. W. Riley (Ed.), *Aging from Birth to Death.* Boulder, Colo: Westview Press, 1979b.

Bayley, N. "Behavioral Correlates of Mental Growth: Birth to Thirty-Six Years." *American Psychologist,* 1968, *23,* 1–17.

Birkhill, W. R., and Schaie, K. W. "The Effect of Differential Reinforcement of Cautiousness in Intellectual Performance Among the Elderly." *Journal of Gerontology,* 1975, *30,* 578–583.

Brim, O. G., Jr., and Kagan, J. (Eds.). *Constancy and Change in Human Development.* Cambridge, Mass.: Harvard University Press, 1980.

Hofland, B. F., Willis, S. L., and Baltes, P. B. "Fluid Intelligence Performance in the Elderly: Intraindividual Variability in Conditions of Assessment." *Journal of Educational Psychology,* 1981, *73,* 573–586.

Hornblum, J. N., and Overton, W. F. "Area and Volume Conservation Among the Elderly: Assessment and Training." *Developmental Psychology,* 1976, *12,* 68–74.

Labouvie-Vief, G. "Adult Cognitive Development: In Search of Alternative Interpretations." *Merrill Palmer Quarterly,* 1977, *23,* 227–263.

Palmore, E. (Ed.). *Normative Aging II: Reports from the Duke Longitudinal Studies,* 1970–1973. Durham, N.C.: Duke University Press, 1974.

Pressey, S. L., Janney, J. E., and Kuhlen, J. E. *Life: A Psychological Survey.* New York: Harper, 1939.

Riley, M. W. "Age Strata in Social Systems." In E. Shanas and R. Binstock (Eds.), *Handbook of Aging and Social Sciences.* New York: Van Nostrand Reinhold, 1977.

Schaie, K. W., and Parham, I. A. "Cohort-Sequential Analysis of Adult Intellectual Development." *Developmental Psychology,* 1977, *13,* 649–653.

Thorndike, E. L. *Adult Learning.* New York: Macmillan, 1928.

Willis, S. L., Bliesaner, R., and Baltes, P. B. "Intellectual Training Research in Aging: Modification of Performance on the Fluid Ability of Figural Relations." *Journal of Educational Psychology,* 1981, *73,* 41–50.

Sherry L. Willis is professor of human development at The Pennsylvania State University. Her writing and research focus on life span developmental psychology and the plasticity of older adults' intellectual functioning.

*Prospects for improving learning and memory efficiency in older adults
are much better than formerly believed, and new instructional techniques
can facilitate realization of this potential.*

Geropsychological Research on Learning and Memory: Implications for Programming

Irene M. Hulicka
Beverley Roberts Gounard

One of the most popular beliefs about growing older is that ability to perform
well on tasks involving learning and memory declines. This belief has received
considerable research support and is reinforced by negative self-assessments
which adults make of their own learning and memory efficiency (see Hulicka,
in press). Given the overwhelmingly negative view of learning and memory
efficiency in older adults held by professionals and lay people alike, it is critical
that those involved in programming for older adults examine the characteristics and actual learning potential of their client population, and consider techniques, both traditional and innovative, to maximize observed strengths and
to compensate for specific deficits that may exist.

A very crucial first step is to examine the assumption that age per se is
causally related to cognitive decline. Most longitudinal studies provide relatively little evidence of decline until the sixth or seventh decade of life (Arenberg and Robertson-Tchabo, 1977). Most of the research indicating cognitive
decline has been cross-sectional, comparing individuals born at different
points in time and tested on the same occasion; in such studies, the results do

M. Okun (Ed.). *New Directions for Continuing Education: Programs for Older Adults*, no. 14.
San Francisco: Jossey-Bass, June 1982.

not permit investigators to disentangle age-related variance from cohort-related variance. Despite an investigator's best effort to match cohorts on obviously relevant variables such as education and socioeconomic status, age differences on learning and memory tasks may also be due to such factors as anxiety level, motivational level, sensory acuity, health status, and medication. Yet, even though this problem, which is inherent in the use of the cross-sectional design, would tend to overestimate age differences in learning and memory performance, these differences tend to be rather small up to the age range of sixty to seventy. Thus, overall declines may not be apparent or sufficiently severe to require the use of special compensatory techniques and intervention strategies until relatively late in life. Furthermore, the extent of individual variation among elderly research participants makes it difficult to generalize from the performance of groups to the expected performance of a specific individual. In cross-sectional studies, mean differences between age groups tend to be very small in comparison to the variability within age groups. Some older adults in such studies perform much better than the average young adult, and the average older adult performs better than some of the younger adults.

Overview of Learning and Memory as Cognitive Processes

Learning and memory involve internal cognitive processes which are governed by the central nervous system. These processes intervene between stimulus input and response output. Obviously, direct observation of the internal cognitive processes is impossible. Inferences about learning and memory are made by observing relationships between exposure to stimuli (such as material presented in a lecture) and responses (such as answers given to examination questions). Persons whose responses suggest that they did not learn or remember material which was presented are described as "poor learners" or as having "bad memories." The assumption is that the cognitive processing of information from stimulus input to response output was deficient, faulty, or inadequate. If this assumption is justified, then it behooves scientists to identify the nature and the causes of the inadequacy and, insofar as possible, to recommend remedial strategies. The "poor learner" and "bad memory" type of explanation focuses almost exclusively on cognitive factors, that is, on central nervous system registration, interpretation, storage, and retrieval of stimulus information. Some of the processes involved in these cognitive operations are summarized in Table 1.

Table 1 is also intended to draw attention to factors in addition to the internal cognitive processes which should be considered in attempts to account for interindividual and intraindividual differences in performance on tasks involving learning and memory. First, for material to be learned and remem-

Table 1. Cognitive and Noncognitive Factors That Might Contribute to Age Differences in Performance on Learning and Memory Tasks

Noncognitive Variables Which Affect the Amount and Nature of Stimulus Input	Cognitive Processing: Learning and Memory (Intervening Processes)			Cognitive and Noncognitive Influences on Response Output
	Basic Sequence	Memory Sequence	Information Processing Activities	
Motivational Variables	Registration	Sensation	Attention	Cognitive
Attention	Acquisition and storage	Sensory Memory	Encoding strategies	Comprehension of task
Ego involvement	Retrieval	(about 20 sec.)	(rehearsal, mediation,	Original acquisition and storage
Interest		Primary or short-	organization)	Efficiency of encoding,
Perceived relevance		term memory	Consolidation (storage)	decoding, search and retrieval
Interference from more		(about 1 min.)	Decay	processes
dominant motives (pain,		Secondary or long-	Interference	Noncognitive
anxiety, security, self-esteem)		term memory	Search	Speed of response
Anxiety		(up to a few hours)	Decoding	Motor factors
Physiological Variables		Secondary or long-	Retrieval	Distractions
Sensory acuity		term memory		Cautiousness
General health		(remote memory)		Self-concept
Intactness of central nervous		Retrieval		Anxiety
system				Depression
Energy level				Fatigue
Experiential Variables				Retrieval cues
Education: amount, relevance,				
recency				
Previous learning: facilitative				
or interfering				
Practice: recency, type				
Learned information				
processing, strategies				
Command of language				
Situation Variables				
Rate of presentation				
Mode of presentation				
Distractions				

bered, it must enter the cognitive processing system. Consequently, consideration must be directed to factors that influence the nature and amount of stimulus input. Among the major determinants of stimulus input are noncognitive factors, that is, factors other than central processes, such as motivational and physiological variables. Second, it must be recognized that behavior, that is, the responses made by the individual, serves as the primary source of information about learning and memory functioning. Clearly, behavior does not bear a one-to-one relationship to cognitive processes which influence it. Response output, like stimulut input, though influenced by learning and memory, may also be affected by noncognitive variables such as physical capabilities and motivational states.

In programming activities that involve learning and memory for adults, it is important to take into account noncognitive variables that may influence the amount and nature of stimulus information that enters the central processing system, and variables that may influence how accurately responses reflect the underlying learning and memory processes, rather than concentrating exclusively on the processes of learning and memory per se.

Learning and Memory: Not the Only Culprits

In this section, information from a broad spectrum of research has been summarized to illustrate the validity of the proposition that at least part of the behavioral deficit that is ordinarily attributed to the poor learning or bad memory of older adults can be accounted for on the basis of inadequate stimulus or response output resulting in an underestimation of the efficiency of learning or memory processes.

With increasing age, there is a gradual slowing of central nervous system functioning (see Birren, Woods, and Williams, 1980). This slowing appears to affect most aspects of cognitive performance from focusing attention on a stimulus through processing stimulus information into long-term storage and searching memory for retrieval of information. For example, elderly adults use more time than young adults to search memory (Anders and Fozard, 1973) and to select and execute responses (Welford, 1977). Given the generalized slowing, it is not surprising that under rigorous temporal schedules, the performance of older people tends to be inferior to that of younger people, nor that the performance of older adults improves under self-paced or relatively generous temporal schedules (see Witte, 1975).

Although scientists have not attended directly to the potential contribution of motivational variables to age differences in performance on tasks involving learning and memory, there is sufficient evidence to conclude that motivational variables can account for some of the observed age-related differences. Motivation refers to those variables that activate, maintain, and direct behavior. Sometimes motivation is conceptualized as variables which push (drive motivation) or pull (incentive motivation) an individual to engage in certain kinds of behavior. Evidence that the age-related deficit decreases when meaningful rather than nonsense material is used or when the learning and memory task is personally meaningful suggests that motivation is an important factor (Arenberg, 1968; Hulicka and Rust, 1964).

In general, the relationship between motivational level and performance efficiency on a variety of tasks, including tasks involving learning and memory, tends to be U-shaped with poorer performance when the motivational level is either very low or very high. Although older people may not be motivated to learn nonsense material, and hence may perform poorly, there is evidence, including physiological measures, that sometimes performance is impaired because of overarousal (Eisdorfer, Nowlin, and Wilkie, 1970). This overarousal quite possibly reflects anxiety associated with fear of failure and perhaps also with the unfamiliarity of the testing situation.

More old people than young people are afflicted with sensory deficits (see Bromley, 1974). Clearly, sensory deficits affect stimulus input, and if there are gaps in the information which is available for processing by the central nervous system, one would expect gaps or deficiencies in the behavior from which learning and memory adequacy is inferred. Likewise, more old people than young people have suffered damage to the central nervous system and have health problems which might lower energy level, decrease pain tolerance, or in other ways affect interest in and attention to specific learning and memory tasks. Pain, fatigue, or anxiety could reduce stimulus input, decrease information processing efficiency, and interfere with behavioral output.

Young and older adults differ on a number of experiential variables (see Table 1) which could affect stimulus input, response output, and the actual cognitive processing of material to be learned or remembered. The most obvious of these variables are education and practice effects. It is well known that performance on tasks designed to measure learning and memory efficiency correlates positively with years and recency of education. More interesting is increasing evidence of a strong learning to learn phenomenon in elderly adults (Czaja, 1980; Hultsch, 1974). Given appropriate practice, marked improvements in learning and memory task performance occurs, and more important, the positive effects of training transfer to other cognitive tasks.

Situational and instructional variables are also relevant. For example, the performance of older adults on cognitive tasks is negatively affected by distractions such as noise and other irrelevant stimuli and is improved if the material to be processed is presented both visually and verbally (Arenberg, 1977; Rabbitt, 1965). Most instructional techniques which are beneficial for children and young adults also tend to raise the learning scores of older adults — for example, active versus passive participation, relating the known to the unknown, and the provision of organizational aids and retrieval cues.

There is some research evidence which suggests that the responses which older adults make may underestimate the adequacy of their learning and memory processes. For example, because of central nervous system slowing, and also in some cases because of motor deficits (stiff muscles, speech impairment), older people tend to respond more slowly than young adults; in some cases, the temporal requirements of the situation may not allow them to respond at all. Further, older people tend to avoid risk taking and to withhold responses if uncertain if the response is correct, perhaps because of heightened fear of failure (Botwinick, 1978; Okun, Stock, and Ceurvorst, 1980). As is true for persons of all ages, responses which would reflect an adequate level of learning might not be made because of fatigue, depression, preoccupation with pain, or for other reasons.

Are There Age Differences in Cognitive Factors?

Not all of the differences between age groups in performance on tasks involving learning and memory can be accounted for by noncognitive variables (see Okun, 1980). Table 1 outlines sequences and activities that appear to be involved in processing information from stimulus input to response output. Since different authors use different labels to conceptualize the unseen processes that occur within the central nervous system, two overlapping sequences have been listed. The first, or basic, sequence merely indicates that attention must be directed to the processes of registering, acquiring or learning, storing, and retrieving material, and to factors which could negatively affect any of these processes. The second sequence which focuses on memory is useful in that it directs attention to research findings indicating that at different intervals of time following information input, different variables seem to control whether the information can or cannot be remembered.

Over and above the noncognitive factors, there do tend to be age-related differences in learning and memory efficiency. Reviews of the research literature generally support the idea that older adults do as well as young adults when given a small amount of information to remember and retention is tested immediately afterwards (see Craik, 1977; Hartley, Harker, and Walsh, 1980). When the demands are greater, however, age-related deficits become more apparent. One of the most serious deficits pertains to memory for information which presumably enters the cognitive processing system with a temporal interval ranging from one minute to several hours previously.

One of the reasons that older adults experience difficulty when they must remember a large amount of information or retain information for a period of time after input could be globally described as inefficient information processing. Older adults are less likely than young adults to make spontaneous and efficient use of mediational, organizational, and deep processing strategies to encode material into long-term memory storage (see Craik, 1968; Hulicka and Grossman, 1967). The less frequent and less efficient use of such strategies results in less learning and less material stored in memory and available for retrieval. It has been shown that the information processing deficit can be reduced significantly by giving older adults instruction and practice in the use of specific information-processing strategies (Baltes and Willis, in press).

Older adults also seem to have more difficulty retrieving information from memory storage than young adults do. Schonfield and Robertson (1966) demonstrated that, at least for some material, the difficulty is truly in the retrieval as opposed to the storage stage. Researchers (see Czaja, 1980) have demonstrated that retrieval is enhanced when retrieval cues are available.

Implications for Programming

This chapter begins with the suggestion that older adults and professionals preconceive of older adults as poor learners with bad memories, and that this preconception tends to affect how older adults are treated and the expectations that they have for their own performance. Hopefully, professionals now know that much of what has been traditionally attributed to poor learning and bad memory is, in fact, due to noncognitive factors which interfere with or lower learning and memory efficiency. The instructor or programmer can affect at least some of the noncognitive and cognitive factors which are related to learning and memory. The instructor or programmer is encouraged to make selective use, as appropriate, of the following suggestions, to evaluate their effectiveness and, equally important, to share with others information about successes and failures and new insights about factors that affect age differences in learning and memory efficiency.

Older adults require more time than younger adults do for all phases of learning and memory from stimulus input to response output. Although research suggests that self-pacing is generally more efficient than temporal conditions imposed by others because it allows for individual differences in speed of stimulus assimilation, information processing, and responding, self-pacing is not always feasible. To compensate for the generalized slowing of central nervous system functioning, material should never be presented at a rapid rate, and older individuals should be given ample time to make their responses.

Absolutely crucial, if older adults are to perform well on activities involving learning and memory, are measures to ensure that information successfully reaches central processing structures. Lighting must be adequate but not so bright as to produce glare. Acoustical conditions must minimize echoes and extraneous noises such as group conversations, traffic sounds, and television programs. The instructor must communicate fully—verbally and visually. Speech must be very clear, not too rapid, and loud enough for all to hear (without shouting) and should be supplemented with gestures. Since a multisensory approach has been shown to be effective with younger people, and has led to improved performance by elderly people on laboratory tasks, substantial use should be made of handouts, blackboard notes, slides, and other modes of presentation.

To maximize input of information into the central processing system, the instructor or programmer must also consider attentional and motivational factors. The apparent inability of older adults, in particular, to ignore irrelevant stimuli poses a particular problem. In addition to minimizing extraneous background stimuli, the instructor or programmer should monitor his or her own statements in an attempt to eliminate irrelevant points. Comments such as "This is very important" might help the learner to sift the relevant from the irrelevant.

Perhaps more important than the external conditions are internal distractors of attention. Because of anxiety, some older adults may be unable to direct their attention to material which they are expected to learn and remember. The overall problem of anxiety and motivation deserves careful attention. Because many older adults assess their cognitive skills rather negatively, they expect to perform poorly. This expectation, which poses a threat to self-esteem and is anxiety producing, can distract attention from the task at hand and in other ways interfere with processing information—even demonstrating that the information has been processed. Approaches designed to enhance self-confidence should be used in an attempt to reduce debilitating anxiety. For example, initial educational sessions, in particular, should be structured to highlight competency and success rather than deficiencies and failure. Attention should also be directed to positive motivation to engage in and perform well on the task at hand. Here, both the drive (push) and incentive (pull) aspects of motivation should be considered. Attempts should be made to arouse the individual's interest in the task, and to provide incentives, either extrinsic (for example, praise or recognition) or intrinsic (pride or self-satisfaction). While it may be common sense to suggest that performance tends to be poor when task relevance and meaningfulness is low, programmers and instructors must take this truism into account in working with older adult learners.

In addition to attempting to ensure that the relevant information enters the cognitive processing system, attention should be devoted to strategies of information processing to ensure that the material is encoded in long-term memory storage and is available for eventual retrieval. Research suggests that older adults tend to make less spontaneous use of active information-processing strategies, and moreover when such strategies are used, they tend to be used less effectively (Hulicka and Grossman, 1967). Further, performance can be improved through instruction and practice in information-processing strategies (Hultsch, 1974). Thus, instructions and practice on processing strategies, including the development of organizational skills and the conscious selection of mediators (associations), is warranted. New information should be actively related to what has been learned previously, or to the older learner's previous experiences. Information presented must be as meaningful as possible to arouse and maintain interest and to facilitate the formation of associations. The instructor or programmer might provide or ask learners to offer associations or relevant examples. Learning techniques, such as simple review, rehearsal, and overlearning of material, are sometimes undervalued and hence underused. Instruction designed to distinguish between major principles which should be mastered and remembered, and minor details which are merely exemplary should both reduce the amount to be learned and remembered and facilitate retrieval.

Difficulties in retrieving material from memory can be reduced by the provision of retrieval cues. Often questions can be phrased to include retrieval cues. For example, suppose that for some reason older adults are asked to list as many plants as possible. Instructions merely to list plants would probably be less effective than instructions which include retrieval cues such as "First, list as many leaf vegetables as you can; then as many root vegetable as you can; then as many vegetables that produce pods as you can," and so forth. In formal testing situations, multiple-choice items ordinarily provide more retrieval cues than essay tests to, though with care, essay tests can be worded to incorporate retrieval cues.

Efforts should be made to encourage the older adult to make the responses which demonstrate that efficient learning and memory has occurred. In addition to requiring more time, older adults tend to be more cautious unless they are absolutely sure that they have the right answer. Care must be taken to reward the act of responding (such as "That is an interesting idea, but have you considered . . . ?") and, very important, to eliminate negative consequences for making a less than adequate response.

A number of other suggestions are worthy of consideration. Because older adults tend to experience fatigue earlier than young adults do, very long sessions should be avoided, and indeed, a brief rest period during a relatively long session might be worthwhile. Evidence that older people require more time than young adults do to transfer and consolidate material in long-term memory, combined with evidence of somewhat greater susceptibility for interference among materials that are quite similar, suggests that it might be advisable for the instructor or programmer to schedule sequentially two quite different activities; that is, instruction in French followed by instruction in art or physical fitness would be a more reasonable sequence than French followed by Spanish.

A final and perhaps the most crucial suggestion is that the instructor or programmer should, in all activities involving the older adult, be aware of the dignity of the individual. This requires, among other things, careful attention to individual differences. Specific instructional techniques which are helpful and perhaps crucial for the older adult with relatively low cognitive competence might be bothersome, inappropriate, and even insulting to the individual with relatively high cognitive competence. All instructional programs should be structured to reduce anxiety about potential poor performance and to enhance self-confidence, without in any way belittling or humiliating the older adult. Laboratory investigators have demonstrated conclusively that older adults have much more cognitive plasticity than had hitherto been assumed. Hopefully, practitioners in their direct work with older adults will develop new techniques to facilitate maximum use of the plasticity or cognitive growth potential of older adults.

Future Research

During the past two decades, significant new information has been accumulated about the learning and memory functioning of older adults. Much has been learned about the effects of noncognitive variables, including motivational, physiological, experiential, and situational factors on efficiency of learning and memory. Fortunately, some of these variables can be manipulated to enhance learning and memory. Likewise, much has been learned about the processes involved in learning and remembering. Of particular importance has been information about differences in information processing strategies along with evidence that strategies are subject to modification through instruction. However, much remains to be learned.

Most of the investigations of adult learning and memory have been conducted in the artificial atmosphere of the laboratory, where, in the main, the materials to be learned and remembered have been selected because of their neutralness rather than because of personal relevance. It remains to be seen whether concepts and principles developed from laboratory research are applicable in total or in part to real-life situations. Laboratory investigators need feedback from persons who work directly with older adults. They need to know whether and how well their principles apply beyond the laboratory walls. But even more, scientists need from instructors and programmers identification of new problems and advice about characteristics of older adults which should be considered in the design of scientific investigations. Those who work with older adults in educational and activity programs encounter a multitude of variables which the laboratory investigator either controls or, in some cases, may not even know exist. If the learning and memory process is to be fully understood and if conditions are to be established to enable older adults to approach their maximum learning and memory efficiency, then the flow of information must no longer be primarily from the scientist to the practitioner; the scientist needs to learn from the instructor or programmer who works directly with older adults.

References

Anders, T. R., and Fozard, J. L. "Effects of Age Upon Retrieval from Primary and Secondary Memory." *Developmental Psychology,* 1973, *9,* 411–415.

Arenberg, D. "Concept Problem Solving in Young and Old Adults." *Journal of Gerontology,* 1968, *23,* 279–283.

Arenberg, D. "The Effects of Auditory Augmentation on Visual Retention for Young and Old Subjects." *Journal of Gerontology,* 1977, *32,* 192–195.

Arenberg, D., and Robertson-Tchabo, E. A. "Learning and Aging." In J. E. Birren and K. W. Schaie (Eds.), *Handbook of the Psychology of Aging.* New York: Van Nostrand Reinhold, 1977.

Baltes, P. B., and Willis, S. L. "Enhancement of Intellectual Functioning in Old Age: Penn State's Adult Development and Enrichment Project (ADEPT)." In F. I. M. Craik and S. E. Trehub (Eds.), *Aging and Cognitive Processes.* New York: Plenum, in press.

Birren, J. E., Woods, A. M., and Williams, M. V. "Behavioral Slowing with Age: Causes, Organization, and Consequences." In L. W. Poon (Ed.), *Aging in the 1980s: Psychological Issues.* Washington, D.C.: American Psychological Association, 1980.

Botwinick, J. *Aging and Behavior: A Comprehensive Integration of Research Findings.* (2nd ed.) New York: Springer, 1978.

Bromley, D. B. *The Psychology of Aging.* Baltimore, Md.: Penguin Books, 1974.

Craik, F. I. M. "Short-Term Memory and the Aging Process." In G. A. Talland (Ed.), *Human Aging and Behavior.* New York: Academic Press, 1968.

Craik, F. I. M. "Age Differences in Human Memory." In J. E. Birren and K. W. Schaie (Eds.), *Handbook of the Psychology of Aging.* New York: Van Nostrand Reinhold, 1977.

Czaja, S. J. "Varying Training Techniques Across the Age Span for a Visual Inspection Task." Unpublished doctoral dissertation, State University of New York at Buffalo, 1980.

Eisdorfer, C., Nowlin, J., and Wilkie, F. "Improvement of Learning in the Aged by Modification of Autonomic Nervous System Activity." *Science,* 1970, *170,* 1327–1329.

Hartley, J. T., Harker, J. O., and Walsh, D. A. "Contemporary Issues and New Directions in Adult Development of Learning and Memory." In L. W. Poon (Ed.), *Aging in the 1980s: Psychological Issues.* Washington, D.C.: American Psychological Association, 1980.

Hulicka, I. M. "Memory and Aging: From Life to Laboratory." In F. I. M. Craik and S. E. Trehum (Eds.), *Aging and Cognitive Processes.* New York: Plenum, in press.

Hulicka, I. M., and Grossman, J. L. "Age-Group Comparisons for the Use of Mediators in Paired-Associate Learning." *Journal of Gerontology,* 1967, *22,* 46–51.

Hulicka, I. M., and Rust, L. D. "Age-Related Retention Deficit as a Function of Learning." *Journal of the American Geriatrics Society,* 1964, *12,* 1061–1065.

Hultsch, D. F. "Learning to Learn in Adulthood." *Journal of Gerontology,* 1974, *29,* 302–308.

24

Okun, M. A. "The Role of Noncognitive Factors in the Cognitive Functioning of Older Adults." *Contemporary Educational Psychology*, 1980, *5*, 321–345.

Okun, M. A., Stock, W. A., and Ceurvorst, R. W. "Risk Taking Through the Adult Life Span." *Experimental Aging Research*, 1980, *6*, 463–473.

Rabbitt, P. M. A. "Age Decrements in the Ability to Ignore Irrelevant Information." *Journal of Gerontology*, 1965, *20*, 233–238.

Schonfeld, D., and Robertson, B. A. "Memory Storage and Aging." *Canadian Journal of Psychology*, 1966, *20*, 228–236.

Welford, A. T. "Motor Performance." In J. E. Birren and K. W. Schaie (Eds.), *Handbook of the Psychology of Aging*. New York: Van Nostrand Reinhold, 1977.

Witte, K. L. "Paired-Associate Learning in Young and Elderly Adults as Related to Presentation Rate." *Psychological Bulletin*, 1975, *82*, 975–985.

Irene M. Hulicka is professor of psychology at the State University of New York College at Buffalo and president (1981–1982) of Division 20 (Adult Development and Aging) of the American Psychological Association.

Beverley Roberts Gounard is a psychologist/research consultant who also serves as an affiliated member at the State University of New York at Buffalo Multidisciplinary Center for the Study of Aging.

Many private and public institutions and agencies provide
learning opportunities for the older population. However,
there seems to be a lack of coordination, evaluation, and sharing.
Programming could be enhanced if gerontologists, continuing educators,
and older people would collaborate.

Scope of Educational Programs for Older Adults

Shirley Waskel

The 1971 White House Conference on Aging publicly and nationally recognized the elderly population's need and right to participate in continuous life-long learning. "Education is the basic right of all persons of all age groups. It is continuous and henceforth one of the ways of enabling older people to have a full and meaningful life, and as a means of helping them develop their potential as a resource for the betterment of society" (McClusky, 1971, p. 6). Ten years later a number of questions come to mind regarding this challenge.

How have the elderly as well as continuing educators responded to this pronouncement? What kinds of educational opportunities exist? Do they meet the needs of the older population? What can be done in the future to provide the kinds of learning desired as well as the best means possible for attaining that learning? By discussing answers to these questions the reader will be given a general overview of the scope of educational programs for the older population.

Age Shifts

One of the major reasons behind the pronouncement of 1971 was the dramatic shift which has occurred during the twentieth century in the United

M. Okun (Ed.). *New Directions for Continuing Education: Programs for Older Adults*, no. 14.
San Francisco: Jossey-Bass, June 1982.

States. At the beginning of the twentieth century the number of elderly totaled three million people. By 1930 the older population had more than doubled. Forty-five years later, there were 22.4 million elderly. It is estimated that in the 1980s approximately 24 million Americans are age sixty-five or over. This represents 11 percent of the population—7 percent more than in 1900, when 4 percent of the population was sixty-five and over. By the year 2000, 12 percent will be sixty-five years of age and older (U.S. Bureau of the Census, 1976).

While the number of elderly has risen dramatically, the educational level has also risen but has not kept pace. In 1952, the educational level of all people sixty-five and over was 8.2 years. This rose to 9.0 in 1975, is expected to reach 11.9 in 1990, and is projected to reach 12.6 by the turn of the century (U.S. Bureau of the Census, 1976). One of the reasons why shifts in the educational level have not paralleled changes in the number of elderly is the high level of functional illiteracy among those seventy years and older. In 1976, 10.4 percent of those seventy to seventy-four were classified as such, while for those seventy-five to seventy-nine, 13.3 percent had four or fewer years of education, which constitutes functional illiteracy. By the year 2000 it is projected that only 2.9 percent of all people over sixty-five will have had fewer than four years of education (Riley and Foner, 1968). This rise in educational level among the younger cohorts of the sixty-five and above age group indicates that continuing educators should anticipate differences in present and future recipients of educational programs.

Projected Cohort Differences

Due to a dramatic age shift, educators will be faced with a much different kind of older person in the future. Currently, older people have less formal education than younger people. This has affected their standard of living, coping abilities, level of health, power base, self-concept, and attitudes toward future education (Crandall, 1980). It has been noted that because of the low level of education and lack of continuous education, the older person today has been subjected to myths, stereotypes, and negative effects associated with aging (Hess, 1980).

The increase in median educational level will result in an older generation very close to the median educational level of the entire population. The rising educational level of the older population will result in a group that will be more sophisticated. Many positive effects will be associated with the higher formal educational attainment of successive cohorts. Since there is a relationship between advanced education and economic advantage, this may well influence the level of health, augment coping abilities which protect the individual against negative aspects associated with aging, aid in decreasing the datedness of the older person's attitudes and knowledge, and increase potential for continuing education, as well as political interest and expertise. The result will be a larger pool of older people interested in continuous learning throughout their later years. This group will be more sophisticated, demanding, and entitled to quality learning experiences as opposed to quantity. They will take their place not only as learners but as teachers, resource persons, and leaders as well.

Trends in Clientele

How have the elderly responded to educational opportunities? What kinds of opportunities exist and do they meet the needs of the older population? Only general information is available about the older learner's participation in continuing education. An overview of rates of participation, needs and preferences, and some of the barriers will provide a limited response to the questions raised earlier.

Rates of Participation. In a national poll taken by Lou Harris and Associates (1975), it was discovered that many of the courses taken by the aged are not the traditional academic courses. For the most part, they are loosely organized, nonacademic, and usually carry no credit. Approximately 2 percent attend or take courses from a college or university. More often, older people are found enrolled in courses offered by churches, continuing education agencies, correspondence-type courses, and workshop-type learning experiences offered by libraries, special-interest groups, or independently as a self-directed learner.

As people advance in age, their level of participation in formal adult and continuing education tends to drop. Johnstone and Riviera (1965) found that participation rates in lecture series, study groups, and discussion groups sponsored by various organizations and institutions was highest in the forty to forty-nine age group at 22 percent. As age increased, participation decreased linearly, with 2 percent participating in the seventy and up age group. Among those sixty-five and over, college graduates (7 percent) were more likely to be enrolled in educational institutions or taking some kinds of courses compared to those who had not attended college (1 percent).

There is no dearth of reasons given by older persons as to why they do not attend. Goodrow (1975), Wasserman (1976), and Graney and Hays (1976) found that from 26 percent to 57 percent of the persons interviewed said that they would be willing to participate. However, while the older population expresses an interest, they do not, in fact, actually participate to any great extend in a formal means of continuing education.

Needs and Preferences. Educational programs provide an opportunity to address current needs and a means of unleashing the potential for continued growth and development. As so often occurs, persons often confuse needs and preferences, emphasizing the latter because the former are not well defined or adequately recognized. Continuing educators often address preferences rather than needs since preferences gain more acceptance and are easier to program. Leading people to become aware of their needs and to then take action in responding to them is a complex process which is more difficult to attain (Crandall, 1980).

McClusky (1974) has made a major contribution in identifying five categories of needs which older people have. Because most continuing educators are familiar with this work, it will suffice to recapitulate the categories and include some examples from each category.

The first of these are *coping* needs brought about by increasing age. These are changes in finances, marital status, position in society, power, health, and occupation. To maintain adequate psychological and physical health, it is important to learn to cope with these and other changes. Through the fulfillment of *expressive* needs, older persons may derive intrinsic enjoyment, meaning, and pleasure. Continued social interaction, the use of the senses, or the use of the muscles contribute to the well-being of the older individual. Also, latent or underexpressed talents or interests held by the older population can manifest themselves. The third area of need is *contributive* as older persons continue to give to others. Fulfilling these needs permits the dual function of fulfilling a useful role while feeling wanted and needed. The elderly also have the need to control the *direction and quality* of their lives. They need to understand how and why decisions are made that influence their lives and how these decisions can be changed if necessary. The final level of need identified by McClusky is that of *transcendence,* which he describes as the need for the older individuals to feel that they are somehow better off or at a higher level of existence than in the past.

Even if we make the assumption that the elderly participate in learning activities which reflect their interests, we must still ask: "Is there a built-in mechanism which fosters a move beyond information receiving to integration and behavioral change?" (See Hendrickson and Barnes, 1967). Perhaps a more pointed question is in order: "Do the elderly want more information?" Daniel, Templin, and Shearon (1977) found that individuals aged sixty and older gave the following reasons for enrolling in adult education and continuing programs: to learn more things of interest, to meet people who were interesting, to be able to contribute to society, to improve one's social life, and to become more cultured. Because these are ranked in order of preference by the older population, it is interesting to note that most of the items given highest priority relate to social and ego needs. Is it possible that while responding to the needs and preferences of older people, programmers and teachers could probe more deeply into short-term and long-term outcomes, to find out whether the information becomes integrated and eventually is reflected through behavior?

Barriers. Because modern societies have segregated education, work, and leisure into different parts of the life cycle, the aged are not considered an important clientele for continuing education. The divisions noted above have created, at least partially, an age-stratified system. Because education is highly age-graded, the new knowledge and socialization that results produce social distance between generations. Our educational institutions remain youth ghettos with both social and psychological barriers for older persons. As yet, little headway has been made in attempting to identify the barriers that prevent older people from attending university classes. When older people were asked to comment on their perception of why more older people do not attend university classes, responses to this question were wide-ranging, with the largest number of responses occurring in the "don't know" category (Hooper and March, 1978). Reasons reported for nonparticipation in continuing education include strict attendance requirements, conflicts between classes and home, too much demand on their time, feeling that they were too old, no interesting courses, poor vision, lack of transportation, dislike of tests, and the ability to learn enough at home (Goodrow, 1975; Graney and Hays, 1976; Harris, 1975). Defective instructional techniques, lack of proper motivation and incentives, along with myths that prevail regarding the older person's ability to learn, also cause barriers for the older person (Harris and Cole, 1980).

Trends in Processes

Programs for older adults are offered by a multitude of institutions and organizations and cover a vast number of topics using a variety of teaching and learning modes.

Providers. Universities, colleges, industry, labor unions, YW-YMCAs, churches, religious communities, senior centers, senior housing projects, government agencies, and libraries all offer some type of program directed toward the older adult learner. According to a Lou Harris poll (1975), many of the courses that the aged take are not the regular academic type courses but are loosely organized, nonacademic, and carry no credit. Approximately 26 percent take courses at a church, 25 percent at a college or university, 19 percent attend school, 10 percent participate in correspondence-type courses, and 20 percent take courses through other providers.

Content Areas. Educational activities provided for the elderly are extremely diversified. They range from arts and crafts, recreation, and tours to more strictly intellectual pursuits, such as philosophy, foreign languages, and so on. To more effectively discuss the variety of programs offered, it is helpful to classify adult and continuing education offerings using Havighurst's (1976) dual category scheme. Instrumental education is education for a goal that lies outside and beyond the act of education. In contrast, expressive education is education for a goal that lies within the act of learning or is so closely related to it that the act of learning appears to be the goal. Courses such as preretirement planning, career development, and consumer-type courses are instrumental in nature and tend to improve the quality of life. Bridge, arts and crafts, languages, and creative writing are expressive in nature and are usually attended because of the immediate enjoyment they bring.

Most of the content offered falls under the second category and does, in fact, attend to the preferences stated by the older population. But as more people live longer, it is becoming more important to address the need for coping strategies which will enable them to live more independently and with dignity. As resources become more scarce, priorities will need to be redefined.

Instructional Modes

Instructional modes utilized by the older learner range from the traditional mode, where the instructor or facilitator maintains control in the teaching situation, through the self-directed mode, in which the learner maintains control.

The traditional instructor or facilitator mode includes lecture, television, videotaped lectures and discussions, slide or tape presentations, and motion pictures. Whether this instruction occurs within a college or university setting or within the community, the instructor directs the student's learning and maintains control (Bolton, 1978).

While the traditional mode is the best known and most widely used, it does not attract great numbers of older people (Hiemstra, 1976). Credit courses taken from a college or university involve the more traditional instructional modes and yet, only about 2 percent of the elderly take these credit courses (Lou Harris Poll, 1975). While a greater number enroll in nonacademic, noncredit learning experiences within the community, many of these also employ a more traditional mode.

Instructional modes which place more responsibility upon the learner such as personalized systems of instruction, programmed-instruction modules, and computer-assisted instruction have met with mixed success within the younger population and have not been used to any great extent with the older population. The most promising is that of computer-assisted instruction. Although, again, this type of instructional mode will most benefit the younger, more educated, and higher socioeconomic groups of older people. Even this mode of instruction is not readily available because of a lack of software and necessary programming. But it is apparent that fewer of the lower socioeconomic, less-educated older persons will be served.

Perhaps the answer lies in self-directed learning. It should be pointed out that the average adult spends 816 hours a year in self-directed learning (Tough, 1971). Hiemstra (1976) found that an average of 325 or 3.3 learning projects were engaged in by people fifty-five years of age and older. Suffice it to say that self-directed learning is an important mode to consider when addressing learning activities among the older population.

Critique of Current Programming

To offer a critique of a new and unorganized phenomenon as educational programming for older persons borders on foolhardiness. To maintain some credibility while offering some food for thought, the author will limit remarks to three areas: relevance of programming, outcomes, and visibility.

Relevance. As early as twenty-five years ago, educational programs for older adults began to appear on the scene. Wilma Donahue (1955) offered a farsighted view pertaining to educational programs for the older individual. In reviewing her prophetic statements, one can only conclude that they are still prophetic and that the state of the art has not caught up with her vision. This is not necessarily negative, since most of the areas which concern themselves with responding to the needs, wants, and desires of the older population are still in the evolutionary stages. But the time has come to ask some of the hard questions regarding the present and future of educational programs for the elderly.

The first of these questions centers around the relevance of the programs now being offered. Relevance can be addressed from at least two perspectives — that of the provider and that of the participant. It can also be discussed in relation to the present and the future. In the past and to a certain extent presently, older people are viewed as having more leisure time. One of the ways this need is met is through the programs of and participation in expressive types of learning. In reviewing the types of courses which draw the majority of older persons, it is evident that they, also, seem to prefer those which are expressive in nature. But more and more, it is becoming evident that there are those who want and need instrumental learning opportunities. For example, as recareering becomes more popular, new vocational skills will be sought by the "young-old."

Because almost all participation by the older learner is noncompulsory, if programming is not relevant from their perspective, they will fail to show. On the other hand, practitioners should not ignore them. They have the responsibility to home in on older adults, to work with them to identify the goals and means necessary to make their participation in educational programs a rewarding experience.

Outcomes. Related to relevance is the identification of the expected or desired outcomes. In reviewing how outcomes are established, it seems that they are closely related to the immediate need reflected by the older person being served. Current programming is more reactive in nature. Viable needs assessments and program evaluations are virtually nonexistent.

While reactive programming does meet some of the demands and is drawing older adults into educational programs, is that the long-term desired outcome? Or, is it time to move to the next step which may seem to some a leap into the unknown? Should there be some continuity in educational programming rather than a shotgun or cafeteria approach? Should educational gerontologists and educational providers be involved in developing a taxonomy which would provide progressive types of programming leading to identified and unified ends?

Visibility of Programs. While the above questions may not be easily answered at this time, they do relate to the topic of visibility of current programs. Assuredly, there are programs available which do respond to some of the concerns listed above. However, these effective programs are cited too infrequently in the literature. It is important that educational gerontologists and programmers be more aware of what is currently taking place, particularly the outstanding programs. Until the myriad of programs for older adults are systematically identified and evaluated, progress in building educational programming for the older population will be slow.

Suggestions for Improving Current Programming

Because it is evident that in the not too distant future the cadre of young-old will be quite different, especially in relation to level of education, health status, and realistic needs, it is important to consider both current and future programming. Also, because the number of issues which could be discussed is far greater than the space available, emphasis will be given to priorities and flexibility in programming.

Priorities. With the advent of curtailed funding on all levels, identifying priorities becomes a major issue. Will it be possible to continue to expand to serve those underserved or to encourage those who have low motivation? Will reactive-type programming survive because of attendance? Will it be possible to be creative in developing and offering proactive programs based on instrumental needs of the older population? Will the young-old, old-old, and frail elderly all be served? If not all, which groups will and with what kinds of educational endeavors? In a time of limited resources, how will programmers respond? Will there be time, finances, and energy to become more knowledgeable about the various older learners' abilities and differences? Will those responsible for programming educational opportunities become more institutionalized? Will they not move out into communities? Will more older persons themselves be utilized as instructors? As outside funding continues to disappear, it becomes paramount that educational gerontologists and continuing educators work together to provide the best possible learning opportunities for the older population.

Flexibility in Programming. Besides traditional and nontraditional modes of delivery and learning, more is being learned about involvement of all age groups, including older persons, in self-directed learning. Tough has defined self-directed learning as "a series of related episodes, adding up to at least seven hours. In each episode more than half of a person's total motivation is to gain and retain fairly clear knowledge and skill, or to produce some other lasting change in himself" (Tough, 1971, p. 6). Hiemstra (1976) found that 50 percent of the projects were planned, 20 percent were group-planned, 10 percent were on a one-to-one basis, and 10 percent had no dominant-type planner.

Actually, it seems that there is, as Cross (1981) has stated, "a propensity for adult learning." Practitioners must nourish this propensity for learning so that older adults can meet both expressive and instrumental needs. The challenge for programmers is to make their educational offerings a part of the repertoire of resources which older adults draw upon as they engage in planned learning activities. As new developmental tasks arise and as some remain important, the continuing educator has a great opportunity to focus attention and concern on future cohorts of older adults.

References

Bolton, C. R. "Alternative Instructional Strategies for Older Learners." In R. H. Sherron and D. B. Lumsden (Eds.), *Introduction to Educational Gerontology.* Washington, D.C.: Hemisphere, 1978.

Crandall, R. C. *Gerontology: Behavioral Science Approach.* Reading, Mass.: Addison-Wesley, 1980.

Cross, P. K. "Adults as Learners." *Increasing Participation and Facilitating Learning.* San Francisco: Jossey-Bass, 1981.

Daniel, D. E., Templin, R. G., and Shearon, R. W. "The Value Orientation of Older Adults Toward Education." *Educational Gerontology,* 1977, *2* (1), 33–42.

Donahue, W. *Education for Later Maturity.* New York: Whiteside and William Morrow, 1955.

Goodrow, B. A. "Limiting Factors in Reducing Participation in Older Adult Learning Opportunities." *The Gerontologist,* 1975, *15* (5), 418–422.

Graney, M. J., and Hays, W. C. "Senior Students: Higher Education After Age 62." *Educational Gerontology,* 1976, *1* (4), 343–359.

Harris, D. K., and Cole, W. E. *Sociology of Aging.* Boston: Houghton Mifflin, 1980.

Harris, L., and Associates. *The Myth and Reality of Aging in America.* Washington, D.C.: The National Council on Aging, 1975.

Havighurst, R. J. "Education Through the Adult Life Span." *Educational Gerontology,* 1976, *1,* 41–51.

Hendrickson, A., and Barnes, R. F. "Educational Needs of Older People." *Adult Leadership,* 1967, *16,* 2–4, 32.

Hess, B. B., and Markson, E. W. *Aging and Old Age.* New York: Macmillan, 1980.

Hiemstra, R. "The Older Adult's Learning Projects." *Educational Gerontology,* 1976, *1,* 331–341.

Hooper, G. O., and March, G. G. "A Study of Older Students Attending University Classes." *Educational Gerontology,* 1978, *3* (4), 321–330.

Johnstone, J. W., and Rivera, R. J. *Volunteers for Learning.* Chicago: Aldine, 1965.

McClusky, H. Y. "Education." In *Toward a National Policy on Aging.* (1971 White House Conference on Aging.) Washington, D.C.: U.S. Government Printing Office, 1971.

McClusky, H. W. "Education for Aging: The Scope of the Field and Perspectives for the Future." In S. M. Grabowski and W. D. Mason (Eds.), *Learning for Aging.* Washington, D.C.: Adult Education Association of the U.S.A., 1974.

Riley, M. W., and Foner, A. (Eds.). *Aging and Society: An Inventory of Research Findings.* Vol. I. New York: Russell Sage Foundation, 1968.

Tough, A. *The Adult's Learning Projects: A Fresh Approach to Theory and Practice in Adult Learning.* Toronto: Ontario Institute for Studies in Education, 1971.

U.S. Bureau of the Census. *Current Population Reports, Special Studies Series.* Washington, D.C.: U.S. Government Printing Office, May 1976, *59,* 9.

Wasserman, I. W. "The Educational Interests of the Elderly: A Case Study." *Educational Gerontology,* 1976, *1* (4), 323–330.

Shirley Waskel is an assistant professor in the Gerontology Program within the College of Public Affairs and Community Service at the University of Nebraska at Omaha. She teaches in the areas of educational gerontology, midlife, and career change, as well as an overview course on the social aspects of aging. She is involved in ongoing research regarding older persons' perceptions of their problem-solving capabilities.

*An ecumenical church-sponsored senior center increases survival skills
and enhances life with programs planned and implemented
by older volunteers.*

Programming for Older Adults: A Church's Response

Paul B. Maves

The Shepherd's Center is the serendipitous outcome of a process that started
in another direction. In the early 1970s, a group of United Methodist clergy
and laity, chaired by Dr. Elbert Cole, pastor of Central United Methodist
Church, set out to build a retirement home in the metropolitan area of Kansas
City, Missouri. Neil L. Gaynes and Bernard Kaplan, consultants hired to
conduct a feasibility study in 1972, observed that "there are widespread, overall inadequacies in available programs of service to the aging throughout the
Kansas City Metropolitan Area at all noninstitutional levels, plus all levels of
institutional service except skilled nursing" (p. 49). They recommended that the
committee obtain a site for the development of a "comprehensive program of
services, [that it] initiate activities toward implementation of a program of a
Comprehensive Senior Center within the existing facilities . . . . of the Central United Methodist Church," and that an Intermediate Care Facility be

Data for this chapter were taken from the minutes of the Kansas City United
Methodist Retirement Home Study Committee, the minutes and annual reports of the
Board of Directors of the Shepherd's Center, records in the files of the Shepherd's Center, and conversations with staff and with volunteer coordinators of program components.

M. Okun (Ed.). *New Directions for Continuing Education: Programs for Older Adults,* no. 14.
San Francisco: Jossey-Bass, June 1982.

constructed, to be followed by a Skilled Care Facility, and finally by housing for the well aged (pp. 50–51).

Shortly thereafter, Dr. Cole submitted to the committee a proposal for the Shepherd's Center. In examining how the proposal and its objectives were formulated, it becomes clear that a number of community organization processes had been going on simultaneously, in which many persons and official bodies were drawn into conversation about the needs of the elderly and ways to meet them. Developing the Shepherd's Center was in itself a learning experience and at the same time one that involved educating persons about the need.

Groups and organizations involved, in addition to the United Methodist Retirement Home Study Committee and Neil Gaynes and Associates, included the Program and Facilities Planning Committee and staff of Central United Methodist Church, the Kansas City Planning Commission, the City and County Advisory Commission on Aging, the Listeners group of Central United Methodist Church, the Missouri State Office on Aging, a men's Bible class (which sponsored a Meals-on-Wheels program), service clubs, the Waldo/Country Club Ministerial Association, the Roman Catholic Community Service Planning Group, and various professional consultants.

The Shepherd's Center was formally incorporated in August, 1972, with its own board of directors. Thereafter, its development was separate from that of the retirement home.

From its inception, the Shepherd's Center was conceived as the ecumenical outreach of the religious congregations within a service area of fifteen square miles, containing more than 12,000 older people. It is now sponsored by twenty-five churches and synagogues in that area.

The Shepherd's Center was visualized as an alternative to institutional care within the metropolitan area. To accomplish this purpose, it was to function as a pilot and a model, assisting other groups of religious congregations to organize similar centers in other parts of the city. This intention is being fulfilled. Currently, five similar centers are operating in the Kansas City area. More than forty communities across the nation have taken the Shepherd's Center as their model and have received consultation or training from the Shepherd's Center Training Service, a separate arm of the Center incorporated in 1974 as the Mid-America Resource and Training Center on Aging.

In 1976, the Columbia Broadcasting System made a documentary film of the Shepherd's Center called "Volunteer to Live," shown first on the "Look Up and Live" series sponsored by the National Council of Churches of Christ. In 1978, GUIDEPOSTS gave the Church of the Year Award to Central United Methodist Church for its role in initiating and hosting the Center, describing the Center in its October issue. Since October, 1978, the writer has been retained to direct a National Shepherd's Center Development program as consultant and trainer.

The history of the institution provides the context for the educational program. We will now look at the variety of educational programs which have been or are now implemented by the Shepherd's Center in Kansas City, Missouri.

Specific Educational Programs for Older Adults

Dedicated to enabling persons to remain in their own homes, avoiding premature or inappropriate institutionalization, emphasis was given first to services delivered to homes of the frail elderly by older volunteers and then to providing learning opportunities which could enhance life by adding excitement, socialization, new insights, and increased skills in living for those who were not homebound.

The objectives of the Shepherd's Center have been refined as follows:

1. To sustain older people who desire to live independently in their own homes and apartments in the community.
2. To provide retired persons opportunity to use their experience, training, and skills in significant social roles.
3. To enhance life satisfaction in later maturity and enable self-realization through artistic expression, community service, caring relationships, lifelong learning, and the discovery of inner resources.
4. To demonstrate life at its best in later maturity so as to provide attractive role models for successful aging.
5. To advocate the right of older people to a fair share of society's goods, and to assist them in gaining access to services they need.
6. To contribute to knowledge about what is required for successful aging and to experiment with new approaches and programs for meeting the needs of older people.

Adventures in Learning. Adventures in Learning, first offered in October, 1972, was adapted from a program developed by St. Luke's Methodist Church in Oklahoma City, called the School of Continuing Education. Twenty-five retired persons, many of them former teachers, made plans for this college-style educational program to be offered on Fridays. The program begins at 9 A.M. and runs until 2:30 P.M., with a luncheon and forum at noon. Every hour, people can choose from among as many as half a dozen courses. At each hour there is something of an intellectual nature such as languages, creative writing, study of literature, art, or current events; something for those who want to explore meanings; something for those who like to work with their hands such as drawing, macrame, and gardening; and something for those who like to sit and be entertained, such as travelogues. Puckishly, this has come to be known as the 4-H Club, devoted to the head, the heart, the hands, and the hind end.

Attendance rose on a wave of enthusiasm during the first three years to a high of over 800 and then levelled off to between 400 and 500 per term. It may be that space constraints had a pruning effect so that, as attendance got too large, people felt lost in the crowd. Or, perhaps, some did not find enough that was new and interesting to continue coming. It may be that burgeoning courses for seniors in adult education programs and community colleges drained off some of the consumers.

A registration fee of $4.00 is charged for each quarterly term. This entitles the participant to sit in on as many of the classes as he or she chooses to and even to sit in on different classes on different weeks. The registrars are aware that a few people attend who do not pay the fee. No effort is made to keep a roll in each class, only the number attending.

As is the case for each program component of the Shepherd's Center, Adventures in Learning is headed by a volunteer coordinator who is supported by a committee. The teachers, registrars, and other helpers are all volunteers, mostly older people. The noon meal is prepared by a cook hired by the church, assisted by a large group of volunteers. Those who do not wish to purchase the meal may bring a bag lunch. Between sixty and eighty volunteers are involved in any one Friday program. Some of the classes are headed by a volunteer who is responsible for the program but who invites guest speakers, also volunteers, in for different sessions. The volunteers are given a complimentary meal ticket.

Each term, persons are invited to suggest courses they would like to take or to name persons they believe would be good teachers. In addition, leaders are always looking for potential teachers. Visiting lecturers as well as teachers are recruited from universities, from public and private agencies, from corporations, and from the ranks of those who are retired. Over the years, the most popular courses have been the travelogues and the international affairs course. Psychology courses are popular also.

The course offering for the Fall, 1981 term is typical:

9:00–9:50. Transactional Analysis, Crime and Burglary Prevention, Bible Therapy, When You Need a Lawyer, Fitness for Living, Astronomy Is Fun, Needlework, Possibility Thinking, Begining Spanish.

10:00–10:50. The Arts, Travelogues, Changes in Our World, Needlework, Macrame, Intermediate Spanish, Creative Writing, Yoga, Conversational German.

11:00–11:50. Money Matters, Book Reviews, International

Relations, Music-Music-Music, Creative Writing, Beginning French, Nutrition, Macrame.

1:30–2:30. Health Enrichment, Intermediate French, Words-Words-Words, Folk Dancing, Basic Drawing, Social Bridge, Beginners' Bridge, Pinochle, Help Resolve Your City's Problems.

Preretirement Seminars. The need to prepare persons for retirement became apparent early in the program. Accordingly, in 1973 the leaders began to offer six-session Preretirement Seminars, with 327 persons enrolled with an average attendance of 200. Subsequently, attendance declined and the seminars were discontinued in 1975. Several factors may have contributed to the demise of this program, including (1) lack of access to those still working, (2) the development of similar seminars by businesses and unions, and (3) the fact that the initial need was satisfied.

Defensive Driving Courses. In the fall of 1976, a series of courses on Defensive Driving were introduced, using the curriculum developed by the National Safety Council in cooperation with the NRTA-AARP. These courses were continued through 1979. They require that instructors be trained and certified before they can offer the course. In turn, those who pass the course qualify for the National Defensive Driving Certificate, which may enable the holder to secure a reduced rate on automobile insurance. Again, these courses were dropped because (1) the market dried up, (2) instructors left the program, and (3) the cost of the course became prohibitive to most persons.

The Life Enrichment Program. Educational programs sometimes come into being fortuitously. Just as the Shepherd's Center emerged out of interest in building a retirement home, so the Life Enrichment Program grew out of an interest in developing a day care center. When a potential coordinator was asked if she would be interested in heading a day care center, she responded negatively. However, she did indicate a deep concern for those older people who had experienced serious trauma from divorce, the death of a spouse, unwanted retirement, or waning health. Dr. Cole urged her to pursue her interest.

Initially she encountered apathy among the clergy, who seemed to think they were doing all that was necessary. Eventually she consulted Dr. Kermit Phelps, a clinical psychologist who had been doing preretirement counseling and who agreed to lead a group.

The coordinator discovered that persons were reticent to enroll in any group that even hinted at mental health or therapy. The persons who most needed it were least likely to attend. She emphasized the positive aspect of life enrichment rather than reconstruction and eventually secured twenty-four members by asking them to participate in an experiment to help others.

The first course, offered in 1974, proved so satisfying that the participants requested a continuation. Attendance rose steadily. The group was expanded to include forty-eight. An advanced group was formed to supplement the basic. In the seven years of its existence more than 300 persons have been involved in the program.

Typically, the program consists of a presentation on such subjects as how to make friends, how to sleep well, and how our thinking is distorted by stereotypes. Members of the group are urged to release their potential. Inspirational materials drawn from literature or supplied by the members are shared. Exercises or examples are used in the presentations. After a break, participants discuss a given topic or task in small groups. Reporters share findings with the total group. Often there is reflection on the dynamics of group processes.

The Creative Workshops. Shortly after the Life Enrichment Program was started in 1974, creative workshops were initiated as a complementary activity under the direction of a retired recreational therapist. The workshops, for which there is a $2.00 registration fee, include such activities as chair caning, painting, and macrame. Registrants pay for their own materials. A fair is held annually in December to allow participants to sell their products. Average enrollment runs between seventy and eighty each term, distributed among six to eight activities.

Health Education. Health education has been a major emphasis from the beginning. In addition to blood pressure checks and opportunities for conferences with a registered nurse, there are exercise groups, instruction in drugs, nutrition, and so on. These are supplemented by an annual Health Fair begun in 1973, which did health screening and at the same time exposed participants to health information and health professionals. The program is committed to wholistic health care, which includes a reason for living and a healthful style of living as well as early detection and treatment of disease.

Recently, a geriatric nurse has been added to the staff. A Health Center has been established at the Shepherd House, where consultations with nurses, pharmacists, dieticians, and others, as well as blood-pressure checks, are available. Support groups such as those on weight control and enhancing relationships with adult children meet regularly. A sixteen-hour seminar on self-care is held quarterly. This program is conducted under the supervision of a committee consisting of physicians, pharmacists, nurses, dieticians, and social workers.

Shepherd House Activities. Each Wednesday a group meets at the Shepherd House, opened in 1979, from 9:30 to 2:00 for programs including book reviews, hobbies, medicine, and the arts. Rather than being a course, it is primarily a social group which designs learning opportunities and activities for itself. Members bring a brown-bag lunch. Television, a reading center, and a game room are available as well as the health enrichment opportunities.

Helpful Living — An Adventure. Persons with handicapping conditions find it hard to participate in the Adventures in Learning. The press and jostle of large crowds may be frightening and dangerous. The Adventures in Helpful Living was designed in 1979 to meet at another church, which is barrier free. This is a small and informal group of about twenty persons. The program is flexible and moves more sedately. Volunteers are on hand to assist those with handicapping conditions. There is a great deal of warm, interpersonal interaction in the period from 10 to 2. Everyong who comes gets a hug and a kiss. Here, too, the lunch is brown-bag. Therapeutic exercise directed by a physical therapist, inspiration, and information are offered.

Training Volunteers

Since 1978, all new staff and program coordinators participate in a four-day seminar, directed by the Mid-America Resource and Training Center on Aging, in which gerontology, the philosophy and objectives of the Shepherd's Center, and management skills are reviewed. Carefully screened volunteers for the Hospice Program receive six two-hour training sessions before being assigned to a family, and then are convened at least quarterly for further study in the general area of death and dying.

Staffing, Administration, and Implementation

The Shepherd's Center is governed by a self-perpetuating Board of Directors, most of whom are retired, drawn from the community and selected for their interest in the Shepherd's Center, their commitment to its philosophy, their relationship to constituent groups, and their capacity to function usefully on the Board. Liaison between the Board and the twenty-five sponsoring congregations occurs formally through a Liason Committee and informally as members have memberships in the congregations. Each of the twenty-two program components is headed by a volunteer coordinator. They plan and implement the programs with the assistance of committees. The coordinators meet monthly with the staff. Some of these coordinators devote almost full time to their responsibilities.

Financing. In 1981–1982, the total budget was approximately $75,000. Four sources contribute almost equally: (1) registration fees, (2) contributions from sponsoring bodies, (3) individual donations, and (4) contributions from service clubs, corporations, and foundations. In 1981–82 an additional $44,000 was budgeted to support the new Health Enrichment program.

Marketing the Program. Programs are made known in a variety of ways. Announcements are placed in the bulletins and on the bulletin boards of sponsoring congregations. Newspapers, radio and television stations are kept informed of regular programs, special events, and human interest stories. Community leaders are invited to speak at the forums, serve as lecturers in classes, and visit particular programs. Two nursing schools assign their students to a month's involvement in the Center, and members of the fourth-year class at the University of Missouri Kansas City Medical School are rotated at the Center for a month. Professionals refer their clients. Word of mouth, in which enthusiastic participants tell their friends and neighbors, may be the most reliable and effective form of marketing.

Brochures detailing the program are mailed out each term. A computerized list, which yields the names of all persons over age sixty-five in the service area, provides over 13,000 names for the mailing list.

Evaluation. Evaluation is rather informal. Programs are judged by attendance and expressed enthusiasm of participants. Coordinators and staff observe what happens to people and make subjective judgments about the value of existing programs as well as the need for others. Doubtless, value judgments determine what programs are or are not offered. Active participation, intellectual stimulation, discussion, and personal interaction are valued. There is, therefore, much give and take, even in lecture courses. Bridge is available but bingo is not. Creative arts are taught but busy work (painting by numbers) is out. Visits to the residences of all persons receiving home services now under way will assess the effectiveness of those programs.

Reflections

Most of the programs implemented at the Shepherd's Center had already demonstrated their utility elsewhere. The exception would be the Life Enrichment program, which not only reflects the unique personality of Dr. Phelps but also represents a new approach to the mental health of older people.

Factors contributing to the success of the programs include a sustained commitment of persons like Dr. Elbert Cole to older people, sensitivity to the needs of constituents, alertness to tested programs that might meet these needs, openness to experimentation, flexibility in programming, a willingness to use and reward volunteers, and skill in community organization as well as a warm *esprit de corps.*

Of course, there are problems. Initially there was skepticism and resistance among the lay leadership of the Central United Methodist Church as well as other groups and agencies. With the success of the program, this seems to have dissipated.

The dependence upon volunteer service mandates continual recruitment of qualified leaders and means that programs are limited basically to what volunteers can do. It is hard to know the optimum ratio between paid staff and volunteers and between professional and lay leadership. Professional paid staff are needed to give support, stability, and continuity to the programs without dominating or taking them away from the volunteers.

Funding is a continual problem. Programs may be held up until funding and volunteers are available. The Board and staff believe that if a need exists and is known, if a solution to the need can be devised, eventually funds will be found. The positive aspect of this is that programs have to be carefully considered on their merits and developed slowly in relation to supporting constituency before being launched and so are less vulnerable to the vagaries of political currents.

As patterns have become established, it becomes more difficult to change them or innovate in response to changing situations. The original corps of leaders are becoming older and dropping out. It will be hard to accept the changes, accept new leaders, and maintain the original enthusiasm of the creators. The hope is that the movement is so well institutionalized and so effectively organized that it will be able to solidify its operation and maintain its momentum.

Recommendations to Programmers

1. Involve older people themselves in the process of needs assessment, planning, implementing, and governing, as well as in supporting the program personally and financially. Enable them to claim ownership not only by helping to plan and lead but by paying at least something for it.

2. Encourage the widest possible participation of learners in the process. Older people need and want opportunities to share their experiences, to engage in reflection, and to be active in decision making. They need to be listened to and understood. This is one of the ways they assimilate new information. Their resentments and resistances need to be heard, too, for in this way they may be testing the validity of what is being taught as well as maintaining their own integrity.

3. Take account of widely different interests, experiences, needs, and motives for getting involved in an educational program by providing a variety of options.

4. Remember that learning is secondary to social relationships. Learning takes place best when supported by a social group which values learning and confirms the capacity to change. A warm, supportive, and loving environment provides the best context for personal growth.

5. Keep in mind that the process may be more important than the product. Board, staff, and committee meetings as well as informal exchanges in the halls—all are settings for learning.

44

Finally, learning and volunteering for service are to be rewarding, exciting,and pleasurable. Older adults are free to choose; they are not likely to select that which does not satisfy immediately. When satisfying, tremendous energy is released and excitement is experienced, for then one is most alive.

Reference

Gaynes, N. L., and Kaplan, B. "Planning Services for the Aging in Kansas City, Missouri." Paper prepared for the Kansas City United Methodist Retirement Home Study Committee, Kansas City, 1972.

*Paul B. Maves is a special consultant to the Health and Welfare
Ministries Division of the Board of Global Ministries of the
United Methodist Church and a staff associate of the Mid-America
Resource and Training Center on Aging in Kansas City, Missouri.
He has authored numerous publications in the field of aging
and adult education.*

*Education, when channeled properly, can become the key to open doors
to a better overall understanding of the aging process to both
our present and future generations of older adults.*

Educational Programs for Older Adults: A Public School's Response

J. Corrine Price

Creative Living: A Way of Life

As a nation we have become more and more concerned with our aging
population and their needs. According to demographic data, there are approximately 23 million older adults living in the United States today, which amounts
to 11 percent of the total population (Fowles, 1978). Thirty-two thousand older
adults are living in Monterey County, California, and about 10,000 of that
total are residing in the Salinas Union High School District. Due to the mild
climate, the clean, agricultural surroundings, and small-town atmosphere, the
influx of retired people will no doubt continue. In general, people are attaining their retirement years in better health, with more leisure time and better
economic resources (Hartford, 1978).

As the older adult population grew, the need to establish educational
programs became more obvious. In October, 1971, the Salinas High School
District offered its first class geared to the needs of older adults. Over a three-
year period, this need became too great for one teacher to fulfill. Recognizing
this state of affairs, the Creative Living Program, under the auspices of the

M. Okun (Ed.). *New Directions for Continuing Education: Programs for Older Adults*, no. 14.
San Francisco: Jossey-Bass, June 1982.

Salinas Adult School, was formed in 1974. The program seemed to grow instantaneously and, within no time, classes were offered in various locations all over the district.

The program has changed as the needs of the community have shifted. Aging is a universal process that concerns every human being. At the same time, the aging process is affected by the social historical context. With these thoughts in mind, we strive to encourage older adults to obtain a better understanding of the aging process. Proactive education becomes the key that can open those doors for present and future generations.

Thousands of retired people find themselves experiencing a way of life they are unprepared for. If they have not prepared effectively, the post-retirement period may be traumatic. The question arises, how can retirees make good use of their discretionary time? The Creative Living Program, offering a variety of classes, helps to resolve that issue. It becomes a way of life, keeping people active and involved in their community. The Creative Living Program is designed:

1. to provide stimulating educational programs
2. to assist practitioners in maintaining independent living as long as possible
3. to help participants improve the quality of life in areas concerning their mental well-being as well as their physical health
4. to encourage participants to become responsible for their own actions
5. to make participants more aware of their own potential
6. to encourage participants to become active in their community
7. to offer courses that will encompas people of all ages and backgrounds and show that the process of aging concerns us all
8. to provide the best possible program for the least amount of cost to the taxpayer and to seek out and work with as many local resources and agencies as possible to avoid duplication of services.

The Program in Action

The Creative Living Program is divided into several units which, together, form an all-encompassing program that tries to meet the needs of the older adult residing in the community of Salinas and surrounding areas. Although emphasis is placed on older adults, classes are open to all people over the age of eighteen; younger students may take a course with special permission of the teacher. During the summer, older adults are encouraged to bring their grandchildren; it is not uncommon to see classes where several generations of one family are participating in the learning process.

Before any curriculum was developed or program started, the potential clientele was identified. As Salinas is located in a rural and agricultural valley, most of the participants come from such a background. However, in the last few years increased migration has created a more diversified and rich community. The modal participant in the program is likely to be conservative in viewpoint, independent with a strong sense of survival, cost-conscious due to having had to cope with the Depression years, may have graduated from high school, has mostly been involved with blue-collar labor (although that is slowly changing), works well with his or her hands, is down to earth, has a keen sense of humor, and takes life in stride. Of course, not all participants fit these categories. New participants tend to be better educated, with many having a college degree (Marshall, Draa, and Price, 1980).

With all of these factors in mind, curriculum was carefully selected and tailored specifically to the population being served. Participant needs are monitored periodically via informal assessments. The various goals mentioned earlier are selectively interwoven into the goals and objectives of each course, so that the learning activities reflect the purpose of the total program. Years of trial and error have shown us that conventional classroom methods and settings may not be best for teaching older adults. It seems that older adults — especially those from a blue-collar background — are more comfortable in non-school-like environments. The whole idea behind the teaching method used in the Creative Living Program is to make participants feel at ease, so that they, in turn, will find out that learning can be an exciting and creative adventure.

Older adults enter the classroom with a wealth of information, and each teacher is encouraged to bring out the resources by using them as peer teachers. Peer teaching places responsibility on the participants and makes them feel very much needed and involved with a total program. It also emphasizes the instructor's role as a facilitator. There is quite a difference between teaching children and older adults. We need to treat older adults as responsible and respected members of our community, and in the classroom, to have them participate in the decision-making process concerning the welfare and future of their class and program. It is their tax money at work, so it is only natural that they have a say in the matter.

It is also of utmost importance to build a socialization component into the curriculum. For example, one can use arts and crafts as a tool to present materials in other subject areas. Older adults are usually comfortable working with their hands and while they are busy working on an arts and crafts project, the teacher can initiate a discussion on other subjects such as nutrition, health, or transportation. It is a nonthreatening way of exposing them to other issues. It is preferable to weave nutrition into a class discussion in the above described manner than to focus strictly on a nutrition lecture.

The Creative Living Program is definitely a community-oriented program working very closely with many other agencies. Teachers are encouraged to invite professionals to their classrooms to talk about their areas of expertise, such as income tax and consumer affairs. Teaching older adults involves more than a subject emphasis. To be successful, the instructor must integrate content with current life circumstances. Teachers are also urged to "jazz up" their classes by organizing field trips, encouraging adults to participate in arts and crafts shows and sales, and to establish cottage industries.

Each participant is responsible for the supplies which may be needed in a class. Classes are offered in a variety of facilities such as a multipurpose center, parish halls, community centers, and classroom space in the neighborhood school.

The Creative Living Center. After many years of searching for the right facility and source of funds, a multipurpose center for older adults was opened in April of 1980. It is the only one of its kind in Monterey County and serves more than 500 learners on a weekly basis. It is totally accessible to older adults and handicapped individuals, as there are no steps outside or within the facility. Bathrooms are equipped with raised toilet seats and grab bars. It is located in the center of a neighborhood with a large concentration of adults residing in private homes or apartments. City bus stops are located nearby and the center of town is only a few minutes' walk from the building.

The center's program consists of several classes that were originally scattered around the high school district in various locations. An integral part of the program is the Rehabilitation Education Assistance Program (REAP). The program was established to help disabled adults facing high medical costs. After long-term disabilities such as a stroke, the ongoing health care, maintenance of good physical condition, and rehabilitation of adults are of major concern. The REAP program attempts to fill this gap in health care in the community by offering rehabilitation services and health information to the adult disabled population at a minimal cost. By providing mental and emotional stimulation in the other classes offered at the center, many older and handicapped adults are able to establish a successful life-style in the community. The REAP program offers students physical therapy, occupational therapy, speech therapy, basic skills, supplementary services for general health assessment and care, and group counseling. The REAP courses are described briefly:

1. Physical Therapy: Exercises to correct physical disabilities, prevent disuse atrophies, and promote functional agility.
2. Occupational Therapy: Exercises for the improvement of upper extremity coordination and strength, perceptual-motor abilities, and general activities of daily living (dressing, hygiene, eating, meal preparation).

3. Speech Therapy: Training for the improvement of speech and language disorders and communication skills.

4. Basic Skills: Improvement of skills needed to function efficiently in home, school, or the community and the exploration of leisure-time activities.

In addition to REAP, the Creative Living Center offers a wide range of special-interest classes, where lifelong learning is emphasized, including painting (oil and acrylic), body dynamics (exercises specifically designed for older adults to promote and maintain good physical and mental health), people and places (designed to "travel around the world" without leaving the classroom), sewing (beginning and advanced), knitting and crocheting, quilting, and journalism (connected to the program's own monthly publication, "The Good Old Gazette").

Senior Educational Activity Centers (SEAC). There are four groups in this program. They refer to themselves as "The Golden Seniors," "Over the Rainbow," "The Sugar Cubes," and "The Creative Seniors." Two of the groups conduct their activities in the Creative Living Center, one is housed in a parish hall, and the other meets at a community center, which is owned by a sugar company and run by the adult school and their students.

SEAC offers a variety of educationally-oriented programs designed to increase student awareness with consideration given to skills, potentials, handicaps, needs, and desires of the individual and class. Students may participate in the following classes: Body Dynamics, Consumer and Community Awareness (designed to make the student aware of their consumer rights), Fine Arts, Music, Art Appreciation, Health (designed to discuss major health problems), Older Adult and Handicapped Resources (students are made aware of all the resources available to them in their community, county, state, and nation), and Personal Finances (emphasis is given on how to survive financially with today's inflationary prices and making the most of your money). All subjects are offered by means of lectures, discussion, films, guest speakers, demonstrations, and peer teaching.

Potpourri, Fee Classes, and Field Trips. Potpourri classes are offered at various locations throughout the district. Courses emphasize that aging concerns everyone and individuals of all ages, backgrounds, and handicaps are encouraged to participate. Not many are left under this heading as most of them have been incorporated in the multipurpose center. There are a few which are offered both at the center and at other locations including:

1. Sign Language: Designed to master the Signing Exact English method by learning the alphabet, expressive and receptive finger spelling, signs, and interpreting skills.

2. Ceramics: Covers a basic background of media, including process-

ing clay bodies, basic methods of handbuilding, firing techniques, glaze applications, other methods of surface decoration, and a historical approach to design.

3. Standard First Aid and Health Safety: Emphasis is on care until professional help arrives and includes preventive and safety measures.

4. Cardio-Pulmonary Resuscitation (CPR): Covers recognition or early warning signs for heart attack and respiratory problems, how to get help through the emergency medical systems (EMS), and the basic skills of CPR.

5. Fee Classes: Offered periodically and can be on any subject matter, such as a short course on stained glass or photography.

6. Field Trips: Offered on a monthly basis for the total program and are arranged by the program coordinator. They are day trips which are scheduled by chartering a bus through Greyhound or Gray Line with as many as forty older adults riding on one bus. In this way, the cost is kept down. Sample trips include visits to the King Tut Exhibition and the Dresden Collection, the California Legislature in session, and a Danish Festival in Solvang. Needless to say, the outings are very popular.

"The Good Old Gazette." This monthly publication, initiated in 1975, is still going strong. The magazine is completely self-supported by student subscriptions and by advertisements. A student is charged six dollars a year if they are sixty years and older and twelve dollars a year if they are under sixty years of age. The editor is a certificated and credentialed teacher and her staff consists of interested students. Drawings are done by an art teacher, while students are encouraged to participate in the layout, putting it together, and going through the bulk mailing procedure. The district printshop takes care of the printing. The publication offers up-to-date information of interest to the older adult, including legislation, either in progress or already approved in Sacramento, issues concerning the older adult locally and countywide, and feature stories on an older adult student and a teacher or other staff member. In addition, "The Good Old Gazette" provides schedules of the various senior centers, recipes, announcements of field trips and upcoming local events, health tips, critiques of books and articles, jokes and puzzles, and much more.

The Advisory Council. The Creative Living Advisory Council, initiated in 1979, is an active segment of the program. The Council consists of eleven members who meet monthly. Their role is to advise and assist the program staff in the development, implementation, and evaluation of educational programs which will serve to improve the quality of education and the quality of life in general of students in the Creative Living Program. The Council is held responsible for planning, program development, communication, resource development, program evaluation, reporting, and program budget. Through bylaws, the Council's responsibilities and limitations are well delineated. The Council's membership is composed of students, teachers, district staff, and community members. The Advisory Council's officers consist of a chairperson, vice-chairperson, and a secretary. Two of its members are also part of a larger Advisory Council for the total Adult Education program.

Older Adult Tutoring Program. For the past year and a half, the Salinas Adult School has participated in a pilot project, under the auspices of the California State Department of Education, to train and use the services of older adults as tutors in English and basic education for migrant workers and their families. The purpose of this program is to help improve the migrant workers' educational survival skills or grade levels, including communicative and computational skills, and to promote greater independence, economic stability, and life satisfaction. Originally, four adult schools in the state were involved. Now there are six, and an effort is being made to extend the services of the older adults to other topics. The older adults have benefited greatly by being allowed to increase their income, but also by doing work that is intensely gratifying and challenging. Some older adults have moved into better-paying jobs after this experience while others have been hired by the adult school as instructional aides in other programs. Older adults, with their wealth of resources and life experiences, make excellent role models. Older adults are also used in this capacity in various units of the Senior Aide Program.

Volunteers. Volunteers are used in assisting the Rehabilitation Education Assistance Program, especially with therapy services. Volunteers also aid instructors in the classroom, either by tutoring, peer teaching or by fulfilling various other responsibilities. They are trained in special sessions with the supervising instructor prior to working in the classroom and also receive ongoing, in-service training. Further, older adults are encouraged to become peer counselors. Preparation for peer counseling in the REAP program involves weekly sessions for approximately six months. Trainees must be recommended by the supervisor before they are used as peer counselors. Peer teachers are those students who have mastered the skills and who wish to share their skills. Peer teaching enhances the self-esteem of the peer teacher and eases the teacher/student ratio. Peer teachers make excellent models and they help to overcome a rigid dichotomy between teacher and learner.

Staffing and Administration

One of the key ingredients to a successful program is the selection of staff. The effective teacher of older adults is a very special breed. When hiring instructors, one needs to consider nonauthoritarianism, sense of humor, friendliness, listening and facilitating skills, willingness to innovate, and degree of comfort with personal aging. Also, if the person does not genuinely care about, and want to work with, the elderly, all is lost. Since participation in all classes is voluntary, older students will spot uncaring instructors and simply withdraw. Under California State law, all teachers have to be credentialed before entering the classroom. In addition, adult school teachers are required to fulfill 135 hours of teacher training over a five-year period to obtain a permanent credential. All staff members must take continuing education units in their areas of expertise. The total Creative Living Program is headed by a coordinator who is responsible for supervising staff and the daily operation of the program, including the budget, curriculum, and staff development. The chain of command is from the Coordinator to the Director of Adult and Community Education, to the Assistant Supertintendent of Instruction and Curriculum, to the Superintendent, to the Salinas Union High School District Board of Trustees.

Financial Arrangements and Marketing

The funds to operate the Creative Living Program come mostly from the California State Department of Education through apportionments allotted to the Salinas Union High School District adult education program. Other funds are obtained through the Department of Aging, Area Agency on Aging, fees, donations, in-kind services (services offered by an agency without monetary exchange or loss of control, in othe words, classroom space and additional staff) and special projects. The program has been in existence for over seven years. To promote the program, all sorts of methods have been tried, and have proven worthwhile for a short period of time. However, in the long run, the "grapevine system" — word of mouth — is the best.

The Adult School and Community Working Together

The best evidence of success for this particular program is that, despite Proposition 13, it still is going strong. Immediately following Proposition 13, many adult schools across the state drastically cut or dropped their entire older adult program. On the whole, older adult programs suffered substantial losses in their average daily attendance. A few of the larger school districts (Los Angeles) were able to maintain their programs (Price, 1979).

The program has changed with the evolving needs of the community and is expected to evolve further in the future. Students are still attending classes on a daily basis and more community agencies are becoming involved in the program. Agencies actively participating in the program include: California Department of Rehabilitation, California Department of Education, Monterey County Mental Health Services, Department of Consumer Affairs, Department of Social Services, Department of Community Services, Housing Authority, Senior Citizens and Nursing Service, Salinas Public Library, Police Department, California Department of Aging, Hartnell College, Salinas

Valley Visiting Nurse Association, Alliance on Aging, Senior Aide Program, American Heart Association, Driftwood Convalescent Hospital, and Romie Lane Convalescent Hospital.

In searching for support for the Creative Living Program, the advice given by Tony S. Carrillo, professor of community education at San Jose State University, has been invaluable: "If you plan to be successful in community education, make sure you get at least thirty different peoople or entities involved. Nobody wants to be classified a failure, so they will back you up."

One of the major problems is the constant search for adequate funding. With resources drying up, it is becoming even more of a challenge to make ends meet. Precisely for this reason, it is of utmost importance to work closely with other agencies; sometimes in-kind services can absorb a tremendous percentage of expenses. If you are developing a program in your community, I recommend that you: (1) take the time to do a needs assessment and get to know the community inside out, (2) make personal contact with the agency's employees you plan to work with, (3) get many people involved in your project, (4) hire the best possible staff to do the teaching, and (5) involve your students throughout the process.

In implementing the creative living program, we took into account the students' (1) background and outlook on life, (2) need for socialization, (3) the wealth of information they bring to class, by encouraging them to share with one another (peer teaching), (4) autonomy, by involving them in the decision-making process, (5) enjoyment and need of working with their hands as a means of opening other subject areas for discussion, and (6) active and full life outside the classroom. Keeping these suggestions in mind, success is likely to be yours if you add two more ingredients to the recipe: patience and endurance.

References

Fowles, D. *Some Prospects for the Future Elderly Population.* Statistical Reports on Older Americans No. 3. Washington, D.C.: U.S. Department of Health, Education and Welfare, Office of Human Development, Administration on Aging, 1978.

Hartford, M. E. "The Need for Senior Adult Education." Paper prepared for the Task Force to Study Adult Education for the State of California, Sacramento, 1978.

Marshall, M. G., Draa, A., and Price, C. "A Challenge for the 80's: Preparing to Teach Older Adults." *California Journal of Teacher Education,* 1980, *7* (1), 65–69.

Price, J. C. "The Effect of Proposition 13 on Older Adult Education in California." Education research paper prepared for San Jose State University, San Jose, May, 1979.

*J. Corrine Price directs the Adult and Community Educational Program,
Salinas Union High School District. Previously, she founded,
coordinated, and taught in the Creative Living Program,
under the auspices of the Salinas Adult School.*

Aging education is more than content; it is a broad repertoire
of strategies and a continuum of processes. These processes are used
to empower institutions, resources, and individuals to respond effectively
to the needs of the older population. Educational gerontologists
are urged to adopt a catalyst role.

The Aging Education Continuum: A Community College's Response

David J. Demko

In 1975, 246 residents of the community college district, aged fifty-six or over, responded to a survey questionnaire asking them to describe the kind of college services they desired. The responses ranged from "We don't want anything" to "Leave us alone." At least two conclusions could have been drawn: either the older adults truly wanted to be left alone, or they believed that education is exclusively for young people. Optimistically, the college implemented a series of approaches designed to provide older adults opportunities to sample college services. For example, twenty-one mini-courses on topics such as self-defense, nutrition, woodworking, creative writing, physical fitness, and health care were offered throughout the community in senior citizen centers, retirement housing, and nursing homes. Over 400 older adults aged sixty to ninety-three enrolled, participated, and enthusiastically looked forward to future opportunities.

By the end of 1981, Delta College's involvement in gerontology consisted of (1) a combined academic and community education student body that was 9 percent sixty years of age or over, (2) nine courses in academic gerontology, (3) six annual retirement planning seminars conducted in union halls and

M. Okun (Ed.). *New Directions for Continuing Education: Programs for Older Adults,* no. 14.
San Francisco: Jossey-Bass, June 1982.

corporations, (4) fifty off-campus courses conducted annually in senior citizen centers, (5) thirty-five annual continuing education seminars for senior leadership groups and agency staff, and (6) an array of forums, conferences, and special events such as senior information days and actual senior proms. This response originated under the direction of one full-time staff member and has been continued with the addition of two part-time associates, and twenty-five part-time community education instructors. Six full-time faculty members located in various divisions throughout the college carry one or two academic gerontology courses as part of their instructional load. All of the above activities are centrally coordinated under the auspices of the Older Population Resource Center.

Principles for Development

Several principles served as both the impetus for initial involvement and continued development in aging education. These principles influenced the nature of our response to the older population to such an extent that a brief discussion of them seems appropriate.

Nature of the Community College. As an institution supported through state aid, tuition, and local property tax, community colleges should be responsive to local needs, problems, and trends. If you accept this notion, then as the community changes (through dramatic demographic shifts), the community college must change. Responding to the needs of the older population, then, was institutionally acceptable, logical, and imperative.

Nature of the College Response. The college response consists of the process of *positioning,* which involves the following steps: listing possible alternatives for responding to identified needs, choosing a response or set of responses, and preparing the organization or in this case, the institution, to implement the selected responses. One common pitfall related to positioning in aging education is being too particularistic, which involves a failure to see the larger picture. An example is assuming that what is needed to respond to the older population is merely the creation of yet another program, course, or service. This pitfall can be avoided by developing a strategy for organizational change, recognizing that organizations do not change radically or quickly. Segments (departments, staff members, a friendly faculty), however, can and do respond to new information, encouragement, and a little help. For example, staff development enables the creation of older population services to occur as a natural and logical extension of the existing college mission and goals. This means developing a counseling staff which is empathetic to the needs of older returning students, faculty willing to adapt to the learning styles of older students, registration and admission staff who are willing to make the extra efforts that make students feel welcome, and so on.

Often, designers of programs have gotten on a bandwagon, borrowing, adopting, or duplicating whatever everyone else in gerontology is doing without regard to whether it is institutionally sanctioned, appropriate, relevant, or, more specifically, has a life of its own beyond its initial external funding. It is possible to avoid the pitfall of being too popularistic by designing for relevancy and passing up the "here today and gone tomorrow" ventures. For example, the use of the college as a meal site for the elderly seems more defensible when it can be incorporated with items such as nutrition education, in-service placement for students, or training for food managers.

Some institutions have gotten embroiled in turf-related issues, leading to fragmented, isolated efforts. To avoid the pitfall of being too hermetic, consider not only the strategy for positioning oneself, but also the strategy for enhancing the simultaneous positioning process that occurs in other service agencies subject to the same prevailing community forces. The staff member responsible for gerontological development is most useful as a catalyst for change. As an internal catalyst, the developer works toward institutionalizing gerontology through staff development. As an external catalyst, the developer strives to gerontologize various local agencies needing to extend generic human services to an ever increasing clientele of elderly. The catalytic role of the gerontology education developer promotes a sense of ownership of gerontology by the college and the local agencies. This sense of ownership enhances the likelihood of sustained involvement in developing agencies and institutions.

The Nature of the Older Population. Successfully capturing the essence of the older population results in the inevitable "gray paradox"; that is, older people are similar and older people are diverse. Typically, the initial response of educators to the older population is to develop a program for the senior citizen which is more social fabrication than fact. Many persons in the later years do not perceive themselves to be old. Yet, practitioners often think about, plan for, and relate to them as old. In short, the successful aging education effort should include responses which appreciate the similarity as well as the diversity of the older population. For example, the individual-needs orientation leads to a response of providing access to existing college services through removal of obstacles related to mobility, finance, and so on. In contrast, the group-needs orientation leads to a response of providing additional courses based on normative life crises, developmental tasks and transitions, and so forth.

The Nature of Aging Education. The previously mentioned principles culminate in a much broader notion of aging education than a focus on content — the creation of new courses for the older population. Contemporary aging education is increasingly focusing on progress. For example, the process of participation (what impedes it, how it can be enhanced) is fast becoming a major aging education issue.

Delta College has expanded the notion of content and process even further into an aging education continuum. The continuum is an emerging conceptual framework which encompasses and organizes the aging education activities of Delta College between 1975 and 1981. The aging education continuum guides ongoing administration and long-range planning. Aging education in the community college consists of strategies related to the participation process, instructional methods, course design, community organization, institutional development, and research.

An Aging Education Continuum

The six-year development and implementation of aging education at Delta College followed a predetermined pattern. This pattern, known as an *aging education continuum,* incorporates basic administrative structure and primary functions of the Older Population Resource Center. The continuum consists of three major functions operating under the umbrella of the Older Population Resource Center. These functions are service, training, and development. These functions are illustrated as a continuum because they represent interrelated, sometimes overlapping, functions, rather than discrete categories.

The Service Component. The essence of the service component addresses individuals' needs through a strategy of access to existing educational opportunities. This is typically an age-integrated approach. Simultaneously, the college addresses group needs through a strategy of developing new learning opportunities based on group (age-related) considerations. This is typically an age-segregated approach.

Service efforts are carried out by the Older Population Resource Center under the auspices of Older Population Programs and include strategies for improving older people's access to existing opportunities as well as the creation of new opportunities. This is accomplished through policies, procedures, course offerings, and special events directed toward enhancing the older adults' assimilation into the mainstream of the college.

The Training Component. The essence of the training component consists of preparation of older adults for positions of leadership, advocacy, volunteerism, and employment through workshops and seminars, professional continuing education conferences, academic gerontology, and a model certificate training program. Training efforts are carried out by the Older Population Resource Center under the auspices of the Gerontology Training Lab.

The Development Component. The development component addresses institutional and programmatic needs related to continued growth through survey research, materials development, model project demonstration, evaluation, dissemination, and consultation. Development efforts are carried out by the Older Population Resource Center under the auspices of the Gerontology Design Lab and include publications, monographs, audiovisual training materials, and task forces.

Service Component of the Aging Education Continuum

It may be recalled that the college's response to the educational needs of the older population includes a two-fold effort. This dichotomy consists of an age-integrated approach (which addresses individual needs by improving access to existing educational opportunities) as well as an age-segregated approach (which addresses group needs by creating new educational opportunities based on common interests of persons in the later years). These two approaches, in conjunction with the provision of community forums and special events, constitute the service component of the aging education continuum.

Examples of college efforts directed at an age-integrated approach via enhancing participation include (1) providing residents of the college district who are sixty years of age or over with six credit hours per semester, tuition free, in courses of their choice; (2) exporting fifty college courses per year to neighborhood locations such as senior centers, retirement communities, nursing homes, and community centers; (3) providing staff development on a college-wide basis to sensitize counselors, faculty admissions, and registration staff to the needs of older adult students; and (4) providing on-campus tours and visitations to acquaint senior adults with college facilities.

The age-segregated approach involves creating additional educational opportunities that lie beyond traditional course offerings. Such new courses are designed on the basis of more or less universal challenges in the later years, such as common predicaments (fixed income, widowhood, retirement), human development needs (based on life stages, crises, and cycle theories), and common problems related to social, emotional, and physical well-being (for example, health problems). The purpose of such offerings is to empower the older adult with the knowledge, skills, and abilities necessary for self-help and personal problem solving. Examples of the special offerings are: Retirement Living, Senior Survival Skills, Older Driver Refresher, Understanding Aging, and Interpersonal Communication Thru Reminscing. The last offering was designed especially for residentially institutionalized elderly to enhance their self-esteem through the use of structured experience, discussion, and informal learning activities.

Retirement planning seminars are conducted on-site at area corporations, labor union locals, businesses, and community facilities. These seminars, designed for employees and spouses, prepare participants for a variety of concerns including finances, laws, health, use of time, housing, and role-adjustment. A variety of instructional techniques (seminar, lecture, self-instruction) and formats (such as Third Age, University Associates, Retirement

Living) are used, depending on such factors as the size and nature of the client group.

A third facet of the service component is to generate community awareness about a specific problem of, or prospect for, the elderly. Toward this end, the college sponsors a variety of forums and special events intended for the elderly, service providers, policy boards, and other concerned individuals. Delta College utilizes the community forums to generate awareness about age-related concerns, to provide opportunities for concerned individuals to interface with one another, and to facilitate the sharing of perspectives, roles, and resources among public and private, formal and informal helping networks. Examples of typical community forums sponsored by the college include (1) Learning is Ageless, a forum on meeting the needs of the older population through community education programs; (2) Substance Abuse and Aging, a forum on the use and abuse of controlled substances by the elderly; (3) Ministry and Aging, a forum for community leaders on using religious organizations to provide the the aged; (4) You and Your Aging Parents, a forum for the adult children of aging parents including problems of aging, intervention, self-help strategies, and resources in aging; and (5) Gerontology Super Sampler, a forum on the significance of an increasing older population for the community at large.

In addition to community forums, a variety of special events are conducted on an annual basis usually cosponsored with local organizations such as labur unions, aging networks, and American Association of Retired Persons chapters. The special events tend to be utilized to promote a positive image of older adults. Examples include (1) the Older Americans Month Fair, which features a talent show, arts and crafts displays, and presentation of the senior citizen of the year award; (2) the Retiree Information Day which features twenty-nine agencies providing senior citizens with consultation on financial, health, education, recreation, and social service needs; (3) Portraits of Aging, a film series for the review and discussion of media related to older people and aging; (4) Health Topics for Senior Citizens, a series of medical presentations by local physicians and health professionals co-sponsored by the local American Association of Retired Persons chapter and (5) The Senior Prom, a formal dance for adults featuring big band music performed by retirees of the local musicians association.

In summary, the service component of the aging education continuum includes enhancing participation in existing educational opportunities, the creation of additional group offerings when necessary, and promoting awareness of aging and older people to the community at large. The desired result is a community college and a community at large (agencies, families) that are more responsive to an ever-increasing older population. And, perhaps more importantly, that responsiveness to the service needs of the older population is carried out as a natural and logical extension of existing missions or roles.

The Training Component of the Aging Education Continuum

Just as the wide range of individual and group differences within the older population calls for a variety of service strategies, the heterogeneity of clientele in the formal and informal aging network calls for a diversity of training strategies. The target groups that the college responds to include elders (as policy board members, volunteers, and paid staff), professional associations seeking to gerontologize their occupational skills, practitioners within the aging network, community service clubs, and public and private agencies such as school districts, health facilities, churches, governmental units, and social service agencies. Typical responses to the training needs of these clientele include workshops and seminars, professional continuing education conferences, academic gerontology, and certificate training programs. Typical instructional strategies include the use of lecture presentation, seminar discussion, and structured experiences. In short, this section covering the training component of the Older Population Resource Center is organized by response categories (workshops and seminars, professional continuing education, academic gerontology, certificate program).

Workshops and Seminars. Community groups frequently desire short-term learning experiences for a variety of immediate reasons: to improve job performance, to acquire greater insight into their own aging process, or to satisfy a curiosity regarding aging or older people. The main objectives of short-term training are to provide general awareness concerning the needs of the elderly, provide skills which can be readily applied to daily practice and living, and generally enhance the ability of groups to relate their resources to the elderly. The Older Population Resource Center provides workshops and seminars, from two to eight hours, on a demand-response basis. Responses include (1) The Older Passenger, designed for dial-a-ride bus drivers who serve the elderly; (2) Communication and Aging, designed for geriatric aides; (3) Psychology of Aging, designed for occupational therapists; (4) Myths and Realities of Aging, designed for families, friends, and neighbors of the elderly; and (5) Making The System Work for You, designed for service providers as well as the elderly. This program informs participants about the availability of resources, strategies for utilizing the aging network, and methods of advocacy both on an individual level for self-help and on a group level for coalition action.

Professional Continuing Education Conferences. The Older Population Resource Center provides training opportunities for professional associations designed to meet mandated continuing education needs. The programs are designed on the basis of expressed needs of the sponsoring group. Trainers include Delta College staff, faculty, and area professionals on a subcontract basis. The training are intended to gerontologize the knowledge base and occupational skills of the participants. Length of the training varies from one to several days, and topics generally pertain to the psychosocial aspects of human aging. Several examples of the conferences follow.

Designed for radiologic technicians, You and the Geriatric Patient focuses on age-related communication barriers, techniques for communicating with visually and hearing impaired elderly, and the designing of institutional environments for frail elderly. Designed for dental assistants, Geriatrics in Modern Dentistry examines the characteristics of typical geriatric clients and humanistic approaches for provision of care, age-related communication barriers, age-related change in dental tissue, model projects in geriatric dental care, and resources in the field of aging. Designed for nursing personnel, Gerontological Nursing: Psychosocial Aspects, emphasizes basic concepts in aging communication in gerontological environments, behavior and behavior change in the later years, perspectives on common problems of the aged, and individual and group approaches to the aged and infirmed. Designed for administrative and supervisory staff on long term care institutions, Practical Gerontology for Nursing Home Administrators focuses on basic concepts of normal aging, communication and aging, and behavior and aging. Relating to the Frail Elderly examines the inter-relatedness of the process of human aging and its implications for communication, age-related and nonage-related barriers to communication, and a repertoire of techniques for relating to the elderly. Designed for program providers, Programming with a Purpose was developed to enable participants to (1) become familiar with the principles of program planning; (2) become acquainted with the concept of programming as an opportunity to meet the needs of elderly clients for new experience, affection, recognition, and security; (3) learn the difference between individual and group programs and the advantages of each; and (4) exchange ideas for individual and group activities with other senior centers.

Academic Gerontology. Delta College provides students and area professionals the opportunity to pursue coursework in gerontology. Students generally major in an occupational program and enroll in gerontology courses for elective credit. Students can enroll in these courses for either gerontology or division credit. For example, Literature and Aging may be enrolled in for gerontology or English credit. Students include a mix of the full-time students, social workers, senior center directors, and older adults. The educational background of enrollees ranges from associate, baccalaureate, and graduate degrees. A designated academic counselor is available to advise on matters related to degree programs (students elect a gerontology track which complements their occupational degree program), course prerequisites, and transferability. A brief description of the academic gerontology courses are as follows: (1) Foundations of Gerontology: the physical, psychological, and social processes of human aging. (2) Human Services and Aging: problems and needs of the older population, current policy issues and services designed to meet those needs. (3) Psychology of Aging: human behavior, adaptation, and psychological disorders in the later years. (4) Communication and Aging: interpersonal communication and the older adult, communication in group settings, and communication networks for the elderly. (5) Senior Center Administration: the Senior Center concept, center structure and functions, and principles of managing a multipurpose center. (6) Literature and Aging: a study of the styles of authors late in their careers and how literary works portray the process of aging and older people. (7) Death Education: an interdisciplinary analysis of the nature of death with an emphasis on philosophical, cultural, biological, sociological, psychological, and legal aspects of death and dying. (8) Educational Gerontology: the need for education in the later years, the role of the older learner, and trends in educational programming. (9) Retirement Education: an examination of problems, issues and prospects of retirement, and tools and techniques for retirement planning education.

A Model Certificate Training Program. In cooperation with an area agency on aging, the college developed a multiyear certificate training program in applied gerontology. The basis for the training curriculum was a set of knowledge and skills established by the area agency as a minumum for all policy board members, volunteers, and employed staff in the planning and service area. The training was provided by the Older Population Resource Center and the certificate was awarded by the executive board of the area agency. The first year's program consisted of six one-day training modules on the following topics: Adult Leadership, Basic Gerontology, Death and Dying, Planning for the Elderly, Rural Senior Centers, and Home Chore Services. Development and implementation of the training modules focuses on content, process, and integration. For example, in the Adult Leadership module, content focused on the essential elements of group process and common group problems; process focused on using experiences such as simulation, gaming, and role-playing to provide opportunities to practice basic skills in group process; and integration focused on problems of, and prospects for, transferring the new skills to the work environment.

The Development Component of the Aging Education Continuum

The Gerontology Design Lab addresses issues related to continued growth on a programmatic, as well as on an institutional basis. Its activities are discussed below in terms of programmatic development efforts, institutional development efforts, survey research efforts, and issues related to growth.

Programmatic Development Efforts. The college's involvement in model project demonstrations has been both proactive and reactive. Our continuing efforts have involved specification of an identified need, development of an appropriate response, implementation, evaluation, and finally, placement of the activity or project. Placement addresses the need to find a method for continuing successful pilot projects, that is, finding a home for them. Depending on the particular project, placement may be either internal to the college (within a department) or external to the college (local Council on Aging, for example). The decision of whether or not to continue a successfully evaluated project is based on several factors: assessing the long-term need for the project, availability of resources to continue the project, and willingness and capability of project host to carry out the project. Examples of model projects include *Quicksilver* (an anthology of original prose and poetry authored by senior adults enrolled in a Delta College creative writing course), Radio Programs (now provided by a local Council on Aging), Senior Forum (a weekly column featuring senior citizen news, now a continuing assignment for a reporter on the local newspaper), Retirement Planning, and Programming with a Purpose (a training manual developed under contract with an area agency).

Survey Research. Survey research efforts have been used primarily for descriptive purposes. For example, a state of the art survey was conducted to determine the aging education activities of Michigan's twenty-nine community colleges. The results have provided useful information to program developers, policy-makers, legislators, students, and aging network personnel interested in aging services within two year colleges. Survey research has also been used to assess needs, to establish perceptions of senior center directors about their practice, and to compare characteristics of older learners participating in age-segregated and age-integrated settings. Results are used in program planning, evaluation, and policy making.

Institutional Development Efforts. As an internal consultant, the director of the Older Population Resource Center is a catalyst for change. This involves identifying and clarifying needs, working with staff and faculty teams for the purpose of developing strategies for responding, providing technical assistance and coordination during implementation, and acting as ombudsman for the placement of continuing responsibility within an appropriate unit. As a result, educational gerontology, whether as a service, training, or development effort, becomes integrated within the institution. Responsiveness to the older population becomes a natural and logical extension of the college mission. To evaluate the impact and success of this institutional strategy, the director annually develops a set of quantifiable objectives with performance measures (how the objective will be accomplished) and outcome measures based on headcount and credit production which are typical units of service used by educators.

Issues Related to Growth. Educators cannot be all things to all people. However, there seems to be a valuable and needed role for educational gerontologists as catalysts for change on a variety of levels: (1) within their institution for the purpose of removing obstacles to existing educational opportunities and creating new opportunities when needed; (2) within the community at large by creating awareness throughout the formal and informal support networks for the older population; and (3) within the community by providing older people with the knowledge, skills, and attitudes to act on their own behalf. Aging education is more than content, it is a repertoire of strategies, a continuum of processes. These processes are used to empower institutions, resources, and individuals to respond effectively to the needs of the older population.

David J. Demko is a doctoral candidate in educational gerontology at the University of Michigan. For the last six years, he has been director of the Older Population Resource Center, Delta College, University Center, Michigan.

*If the educational provider makes appropriate use of the
Commission on Aging's Services, it can help significantly
in efforts to develop educational programs for older adults.*

Providing Education for Older Adults: A County Commission on Aging's Perspective

Lev E. Levenson

Provision of educational opportunities for older adults as part of a county-wide effort is very complex. The results reflect many influences, not the least of which is the role played by a county commission on aging. This chapter describes commission activities and suggests ways in which continuing education providers can work together with a commission to enhance educational opportunities for older adults.

Transactions between a commission and providers of educational activities for older adults occur with the context of the larger community. Each provider affects and is affected by other providers and by the commission. As a staff member of the commission on aging, I have a unique perspective on the range of educational services and agencies that serve older people. This perspective enables me to analyze relationships between the commission on aging and various continuing education providers. In this chapter, I describe how the Dane County, Wisconsin, Commission on Aging works with local providers. Then I highlight some of the most salient issues for continuing education providers.

M. Okun (Ed.). *New Directions for Continuing Education: Programs for Older Adults*, no. 14.
San Francisco: Jossey-Bass, June 1982.

The Dane County Effort

Data from a long range plan for elderly residents of Dane County indicate that in 1980 the population of people sixty-five and older was 26,489, and that during the next decade this group will increase by 14.6 percent to 30,375 people. Census figures for 1970 (the latest available at the time of the preparation of the plan) indicated that 66 percent of the elderly in the county lived in urban population centers of over 3,500. The older resident of the county tends to be better educated, more urban, and more comfortable economically than the elderly in either the state of Wisconsin or the nation as a whole (Committee on Long Range Planning for the Elderly of Dane County, 1982). This is largely because the state capital, the University of Wisconsin–Madison, and a number of insurance company headquarters are located in the county. The area's farmland is also rich and productive, leading to a somewhat prosperous rural population.

In December, 1972, the Dane County Board of Supervisors established the Dane County Commission on Aging as the focal point of services that address the needs and concerns of older people in the county. The activities of the Commission on Aging are reflected in the mission statement that serves as the framework for the Commission's planning role. It is charged to "develop and implement programs and services designed to meet the changing needs of an increased number of older persons in Dane County, to enhance their dignity and well-being and promote their independence and involvement in the community" (Dane County Commission on Aging, 1982, p. 7). As director of the Lifelong Learning Program, I am responsible for carrying out the educational plans and policies of the Commission. These responsibilities include serving as a consultant to local providers, making resources and support available, and providing information about learning opportunities for older people.

The total educational effort for the elderly in the county consists of the Commission on Aging, with its Lifelong Learning Program staff, and a number of local educational providers. Their interrelationships and the environment within which they function are important considerations. The educational providers in the county vary in size, funding, programs offered, autonomy, staff, and other factors. A 1982 directory of resources for the county's older residents lists twenty-four providers whose responsibilities are primarily or largely educational. A number of other providers listed include learning programs as one component of their service to the elderly (Dane County Aging Program, 1982). Many of the providers are independent of the Commission on Aging; other providers are funded by the Commission and are under its administrative influence.

A major responsibility of the Commission on Aging is planning for services of all kinds to older residents of the county. In 1979, the Commission on

Aging formulated a plan within guidelines developed by the Wisconsin Bureau of Aging. This plan, and subsequent ones, specified the role of the Commision on Aging in providing educational programs and related this role to larger goals of service (Dane County Commission on Aging, 1980, 1981, 1982).

The service plan of the Lifelong Learning Program is included in the annual plan. The following statement of philosophy guides the Program's response to the county's educational system for older people: "Recognizing that being human is a process of continuing development, the Dane County Commission on Aging believes that continued learning is a critical requisite of successful aging. Because of this, the individual should have mental stimulation, the opportunity to exercise esthetic and physical senses, and through meaningful learning experiences, continue personal growth and development, thus ensuring psychological and social well-being" (Dane County Commission on Aging, 1982, p. 80).

In 1981, the Commission on Aging received support from the National Association of Counties Research, Inc., that enabled Dane County to engage in long range planning for the elderly. A twenty-year plan, *Dane County's Elderly, 1981–2000: Confronting the Challenge* (Committee on Long Range Planning for the Elderly of Dane County, 1982), was developed to aid service providers and agencies, as well as governmental bodies, in addressing the concerns of older people. It summarizes major issues that the county and its older population will face in the coming years. The section on Lifelong Learning details eight global issues and needs and provides recommendations regarding how local providers of educational activities for older adults can help meet these needs.

The Commission on Aging varies in its influence on educational providers. The county has many providers that are independent of the Commission's authority. These include institutions such as the University of Wisconsin–Madison, the district vocational and technical college, and local colleges and school systems. Other independent providers include churches, nursing homes, social service agencies, hospitals, and so on. A smaller number of providers funded by the Commission on Aging are under partial administrative control. Examples of these providers include a unique program that offers classes taught by professional writers and artists, the educational component of multipurpose senior centers, some community learning centers for older people, and the nutrition education program offered through Title III congregate meal sites.

Many providers—both independent and funded—share and exchange ideas and resources. They work toward common goals by serving together on committees, advisory groups, and organizations. This activity is strongly supported by the Commission on Aging, which tries to promote a comprehensive and integrated system of educational programs and providers.

The Advisory Council to the Lifelong Learning Program offers opportunities for representatives of providers and older learners to express their needs to the Commission on Aging and to work together to the benefit of the provider and the learner. Another aspect of cooperation is found in the provision of special classes by independent agencies (such as the vocational and technical college or the public schools) located in senior centers funded by the Commission on Aging.

Program initiation is a responsibility shared by the Commission on Aging and other providers in the county. The most important illustration of this to date has been the establishment of model demonstration community learning centers for older adults (Faye McBeath Institute on Aging and Adult Life, 1978). This project began with an idea generated by an educational advisory group to the Commission on Aging. The model learning centers have served as the impetus for a coalition of older adults and service providers to open a new learning center in an existing senior center. The Commission on Aging's financial support to the learning centers enabled them to continue in operation past the completion of the demonstration project, until they generated sufficient local funding.

In the 1982 *Plan* (Dane County Commission on Aging, 1982), the Commission instituted a stronger program of service to the institutionalized older person, recognizing the need of this group for increased educational opportunities. Earlier contacts of the Lifelong Learning Program Director with nursing home staff indicated that they would welcome aid in providing increased educational services to the residents; the residents also exppressed a desire to the Commission on Aging for further learning opportunities.

Coordinating services with the county through Commission activities helps ameliorate the significant barrier that distance poses to the older learner. Multipurpose senior centers are strategically located geographically to provide regional service. Because of the variety of programs at the senior center, it is an excellent site for educational activities. The senior center frequently does its own educational programming. Several senior centers conduct the Senior Center Humanities Program discussion groups through the support of the Lifelong Learning Program, and many senior centers house programs offered by other educational providers.

The Commission's commitment to planning and coordination is carried out via support services as well as funding. Primary support is given to the provider by the Lifelong Learning Program staff's consultation on topics necessary to the design and administration of educational activities for the elderly. The Commission offers workshops on administrative matters to service providers. The Lifelong Learning Program staff works with other staff of the Aging Program to present workshops. They are taught by staff or by contracted consultants. The Lifelong Learning Program is a central clearinghouse that provides access to resource material, teachers, and program ideas. It has been designated as the regional repository for the Senior Center Humanities Program discussion materials by the National Council on Aging. The Lifelong Learning Program Staff distributes the materials, coordinates the programs in the county, helps to start new groups, and trains discussion leaders.

County-Wide Educational Opportunities for Older Learners

The experience of the Dane County Commission on Aging and the theoretical framework of general systems theory provides the perspective presented in this section (Bertalanffy, 1968). The conceptualization suggests how providers can work with a county commission on aging.

The commission performs three main functions: planning, coordinating, and supporting. Planning includes initiating and setting goals and directions. The planners are guided by conscious and deliberate design efforts in seeking the best alternatives to reach desired educational goals. The plan identifies needs and concerns, initiates programs, sets funding priorities, directs resource allocation, and establishes standards for program administration. The commission's annual and long-range plans provide a guiding framework for providers in the development of their individual service plans.

Providers influence the commission's planning efforts by contributing data about local conditions, client needs and desires, ways in which the provider can meet community concerns, available resources, and barriers to accomplishing goals. The provider should be aware that the commission plans for the entire county. Local interests may be incorporated into the plan, but the commission may also set other priorities for the county's educational effort.

Coordination brings the resources of several providers together so they may be integrated to meet common goals. The commission's coordinating activities include:

1. Establishing groups of providers to share ideas, information, experiences, plans, and so forth, and to avoid unnecessary duplication of effort,
2. Directing clients to programs that meet specific needs or interests,
3. Linking providers with other agencies in the aging network so that they can cooperate to address multiple client concerns,
4. Providing program information of all kinds in an easily accessed central location,
5. Bringing the provider and other community agencies and services together in a cooperative manner.

The commission funds providers that meet the priorities and guidelines established by the county-wide service plan. Contracts based on proposals developed by the provider enable the commission to influence program administration by having the provider meet expressed requirements. Providers are also given assistance in obtaining funding from other sources by aid in writing grant proposals, organizing grass-roots fund raising campaigns, and by the commission's service as an intermediary between the provider and alternate funding sources.

Other aspects of the support function carried out by staff activities include giving the provider information about needs assessments and data gathering procedures; advising in program design, implementation and evaluation; locating resource people and teachers; and providing public relations material. The staff does this by individual consultations with providers and by conducting workshops and in-service programs for groups of providers. Staff members also work with older people in the community so they can assume positions of leadership in the educational program.

The commission initiates programs, or stimulates providers to begin programs, based on data gathered during the planning process. The countywide perspective of the commission enables it to respond to educational needs, special target populations, and services that might otherwise not be addressed. Programs initiated by the commission are then turned over to the provider for continuation. The commission financially supports the program until it becomes self-sufficient.

These activities are exercised within an organizational structure that is largely dependent upon relationships between the commission and the providers. Five relationships may be identified: (1) hierarchical, (2) parallel, (3) cooperative, (4) responsive, and (5) conflictual. These relationships are not mutually exclusive.

In a *hierarchical* relationship, the commission influences providers through contractual agreements. The other four types of relationships are between the commission and independent providers. *Parallel* relationships exist between the commission and autonomous providers that offer educational programs to older adults. These may be major institutions, such as colleges and universities, public school systems, or libraries; or they may be smaller efforts such as those within churches or housing units for the elderly. These providers and the educational components of agencies funded by the commission — senior centers or respite care service agencies, for example — can enter into *cooperative* relationships without losing program or administrative autonomy. Identifications of an educational need, and the mobilization of a provider to meet that need establishes a *responsive* relationship. The commission's long-range planning activities promote this relationship.

Conflictual relationships are present when the commission and the provider are in substantial disagreement about some significant aspect of the system for providing educational opportunities for older learners. The resolution of the conflict can frequently benefit the system by enhancing the provision of these programs.

The environment exerts a potent force on the system. Some of the more important environmental constraints identified include population density, geographic location of clients, transportation, community attitudes about education for the elderly, and the presence of noneducational programs and services in the community. The attitudes and relationships of adjoining municipalities may also block cooperative efforts. Special efforts, such as funding transportation services, and mediating disputes among other governmental bodies help ameliorate these barriers.

Issues and Concerns

From the perspective of the commission, issues may be divided into administrative conflicts and concerns about the educational program. Administrative conflicts may develop because of the potential for misuse of the commission's power. Concerns about the educational program involve many specific issues, only some of which will be touched upon.

The core conflict is between local autonomy versus central control. Providers fear that the commission's implementation of its charge results in loss of control over their programs. This concern is particularly acute among providers in a hierarchical relationship to the commission, but it is also shared by smaller, less powerful independent providers. The anxiety is exacerbated by the commission's funding role, and contractual requirements that are placed on providers.

The commission attempts to deal with this fear by distinguishing between administrative requirements and program guidelines. Administrative requirements are necessary for program and financial accountability. Program guidelines provide direction regarding the involvement of older people in leadership roles, data gathering for program development, cooperative efforts on the part of the provider, sensitivity and responsiveness to community needs, and the like. Through these guidelines, the commission works to improve program quality and to further the coordination of the county-wide effort.

Concerns about program provision originate in the educational activities of the provider. Some clients continually express a desire for more recreational activities; other clients argue for additional educational programs. The provider desires to accommodate these conflicting demands, but frequently cannot do so because of insufficient resources, program time, staff, or other considerations. Adapting programs to clients who present diverse interests, needs, and educational and cultural backgrounds is often difficult. In addition, tensions develop in the need for sophisticated staff and the desire to develop leadership among older people so they may design and provide their own programs.

The commission can act to reduce these stresses on the provider by educating older people to take positions of leadership. Consultation with providers and clients help them resolve conflicts over program content. Support

74

services provided by commission staff ease the burden of the provider in coping with these problems and help in adapting services to individual differences among clients.

Summary

An overview has been presented of a county-wide educational effort for older learners. The description of the Dane County Commission on Aging and the more general conceptualization indicate the type of activities performed by the commission.

The commission's activities include planning and setting county-wide priorities, coordinating the work of providers, and funding and supporting providers' educational programs. The commission's staff offers information, consultation and training to the provider so as to help improve program quality and reduce difficulties in program operation. In so doing, the commission attempts to facilitate the offering of educational activities for the older adult learner. One major area of potential conflict, particularly with programs that it funds, is ownership and control over how the programs are implemented.

References

Bertalanffy, L. von. *General Systems Theory.* New York: George Braziller, 1968.

Committee on Long Range Planning for the Elderly of Dane County. *Dane County's Elderly, 1981-2000: Confronting the Challenge.* Madison, Wisc.: Dane County Aging Program, 1982.

Dane County Aging Program. *Activities, Services, and Senior Discounts Available to People in Dane County Who Are Over 60.* Madison, Wisc.: Dane County Aging Program, 1982.

Dane County Commission on Aging. *1980 Plan for Older People: Dane County Commission on Aging's Response to Concerns and Views of Older People.* Madison, Wisc.: Dane County Commission on Aging, 1980.

Dane County Commission on Aging. *1981 Plan for Older People.* Madison, Wisc.: Dane County Commission on Aging, 1981.

Dane County Commission on Aging. *1982 Plan for Older People.* Madison, Wisc.: Dane County Commission on Aging, 1982.

Faye McBeath Institute on Aging and Adult Life, University of Wisconsin–Madison. *"Community-Based Learning Centers for Older Adults Demonstration Project" Project Proposal.* Madison, Wisc.: The Faye McBeath Institute on Aging and Adult Life, 1978.

Lev. E. Levenson is director of the Lifelong Learning Program of the Dane County Program on Aging. He received his doctorate in Library Science from the University of Wisconsin–Madison and has done postdoctoral work in adult education and human development. He has been a public library administrator and has been on the faculty of the University of Wisconsin–Oshkosh.

*Continued growth of educational programming for older people
will depend on the decisions which are made regarding several issues
facing the field.*

Issues in Educational
Programming for Older Adults

*David A. Peterson
Rosemary A. Orgren*

As the preceding chapters attest, educational programming for older people
has grown rapidly in the past three decades. Continued expansion is expected
because the contemporary social context strongly supports both individual
learning and educational programming. On the one hand, the increasing
number of older people and their receptivity to educational offerings make
them an attractive clientele, while, on the other hand, many developments in
contemporary American society encourage educational participation.

The older population will continue to expand, at least until 2030. The
increasing numbers as well as the rising percentage of persons over age sixty-
five provide more potential clients for instructional programs. This potential is
expected to become reality because persons reaching later maturity in the future will have higher levels of formal education, are more likely to have been
participants in adult education, have higher socioeconomic status, and have
better health — all variables which are positively related to educational participation (Palmore, 1976). Thus, future cohorts of older people will be more in-
clined to participate in educational activities and will be more discriminating
consumers of education than their predecessors.

Likewise, social change in America has created a supportive climate for
older adult education. This reflects a national movement toward the creation

M. Okun (Ed.). *New Directions for Continuing Education: Programs for Older Adults*, no. 14.
San Francisco: Jossey-Bass, June 1982.

of a learning society — a cultural environment in which lifelong learning has become widespread and education is used as a way of more adequately adjusting to personal and social change (Aslanian and Brickell, 1980; Cross, 1981). This cultural and social growth has been allowed by the great economic productivity of our nation which supports many nonemployed individuals.

Other contemporary developments, such as the declining number of children and young adults, are encouraging educational institutions to recruit new clientele, older people being identified as one undereducated group. As older people turn to education and instructional programming grows, a variety of issues are raised about the most effective means of organizing and providing learning activities. Although these issues are increasingly recognized today, there is little evidence that they are being adequately addressed by educational providers or policy makers.

The Purpose of Educational Programs for Older Persons

The older population is diverse, therefore instruction designed to meet their needs and interests must show significant variety in educational purpose. However, as public and philanthropic funds are insufficient to support every possible purpose, some determination of priorities is required. This will mandate difficult decisions as many equally valid contents, emphases, and outcomes vie for acceptance. Three basic questions come to mind:

1. Is the purpose of education to assist older people in adjusting to contemporary society or is it to provide them skills and encouragement to remake society to their desires? Contemporary instructional programming has emphasized coping and instrumental strategies, implicitly opting for personal adjustment. It is equally defensible, however, to assist older persons in identifying unacceptable social conditions and developing the advocacy skills to rectify them. When adjustment is selected as the purpose of instruction, educational programming easily becomes the tool of society to maintain the status quo, while the advocacy approach places the programmer in the position of challenging contemporary social arrangements. As new cohorts reach age sixty-five, they are likely to evidence increasing militancy if they find themselves disadvantaged; thus educational programmers may be forced to assume a leading role or be cast aside as irrelevant to the major issues of the day.

2. Does educational programming have the greatest impact when it is content-oriented or when it is process oriented? Most instruction for older people is designed to transmit substantive content; little of it consciously encourages examination of the learning process and increases learning skills. We continue to teach content to people who are not effective learners rather than offering study skills, memory techniques, and learning approaches which can be used in numerous educational settings. Until emphasis is placed on the de-

velopment of learning skills, we will never create a nation of independent learners.

3. Is the purpose of educational programming to serve the needs and interests of voluntary participants or to seek out the undereducated person, the would-be learner, and the individual who has failed to express interest in further learning? At the present time, most programming caters to those who voluntarily participate. So long as this continues, the educational gap between the highest socioeconomic level and the lowest will widen, and education for older people will serve the elite rather than the disadvantaged—a condition which is not likely to encourage appropriation of public or philanthropic funds.

These three questions can be collapsed into one general issue: Should the purpose of educational programming for older people be to maintain the status quo, or should it be the instrument of change? Program planners currently show little inclination to assume a change-agent role, and perhaps this is appropriate. The implication, however, is that persons and resources seeking to improve the quality of life for the disadvantaged will not be recruited to this area, and it will be difficult to build a rationale that educational programs are truly improving society.

The Content of Educational Programming

Education is typically content-oriented; that is, the material to be taught is the principal attribute of the instruction. If a student or faculty member is asked to describe a course, they typically reply in terms of the content rather than commenting upon the institution, method, clientele, or purpose. Consequently, the content offered to older students presents a second substantive issue for the future, not as an attempt to determine one particular content area, but in deciding who will choose the content to be offered.

As voluntary education, instruction for older people has emphasized content which is appealing to this clientele. Courses in recreation, hobby areas, religion, current events, travel, and adjustment to retirement are generally perceived as desired; consequently, they are widely offered. This strategy has succeeded in increasing program enrollment and has proven sufficient to maintain course attendance.

There are, however, a variety of alternative program emphases that are also valuable. These include retraining, degree programs, learning skills, advocacy techniques, or scientific instruction—topics which are perceived to be less attractive, thus drawing fewer enrollments. Content decisions have been removed from the control of the educational programmer and placed in the hands of the client. This raises serious questions:

1. Should educational institutions offer a comprehensive program of

instruction or limit the content to clientele preferences? If educational programmers are successful in assessing the real problems of the community and designing educational programs to meet these needs, society and the individual benefit. This forms a sound rationale for public support of the programs and results in the program being highly valued. However, if the wishes of the clientele dictate which programs will be offered, there is little likelihood of recruiting those who have failed to participate in the past or of making serious impact on the community. Consequently, little can be expected in the way of public support, financial or moral. It is a question of whether the offerings should form a cafeteria of learning opportunities with the patron determining if a balanced meal is desired, or whether the dietician (programmer) should set out a plate containing an appetizing and balanced diet. To date, we have opted for the cafeteria approach, but the residue of this decision has been low status, limited resources, and small attendance.

2. Who is the beneficiary of the educational programming? If we assume that education for older persons is a voluntary activity which may be of interest to some persons and not to others, then those who choose to participate are most likely to benefit. However, if education is to play a role in integrating older people into society, developing equity among age cohorts, raising social consciousness, or promoting a variety of other social values, then the benefit to the entire population increases with the extent of participation. If the content can be tailored so that it appeals to all, it will have a much greater impact. Thus, decisions about content and format will influence to whom the benefits accrue.

The issue of content can be summarized into the dichotomy between the public good and the individual good. If we want the best for everyone, then some overall content plan seems best. If the content is to help the individual in the way he or she wishes to be helped, then a laissez-faire system of "let the market decide" should be maintained.

Methods of Educating Older Persons

Laboratory research on intelligence and learning suggests many guides for the concerned instructor. However, use of them is dependent upon whether the older learners are segregated from or integrated with learners of other ages and whether the learning takes place in a classroom or through some type of mediated instruction.

There is no best instructional method to be used with all older learners in all settings. We have yet to discover any universal panacea. However, much is known about applying various types of instruction to different groups of learners. This knowledge raises several questions about its application:

1. Should instruction be provided to older people on an age-integrated

or age-segregated basis? If older people are formed into age-homogeneous groups, then there are many suggestions which can facilitate effective learning. On the other hand, if intergenerational instruction is provided, then greater knowledge is needed to assure than the instructional methods selected apply equally to all. Too often, age-integrated instruction means that traditional methods are chosen, methods which disadvantage other people, frequently forcing them out of the setting.

Older learners generally prefer to learn in groups of their own age peers rather than in intergenerational settings. The cause of this preference is unclear, but some change will be needed if multigenerational learning is to become widespread.

2. Should instructional methods for older persons be formal or informal? To a degree, this is a repetition of the preceding question because intergenerational learning typically means that traditional pedagogical methods are employed. Age-integrated classes offer only the choice of a formal classroom, with rigorous curriculum and instruction domination. Informal instruction, alternatively, is more frequently used in senior adult education and offers less pressure, slower pace, greater socialization, and student direction. The informal approach is preferred by older persons, but causative variables (age, formality, and method) are difficult to assess.

The methods of instruction will determine the receptivity of older people to education and the effectiveness of the learning. This issue, then, contrasts the extent to which the traditional classroom mode can be successfully utilized by older people in combination with younger learners and the advantages which might come from age-segregated, informal instruction. The latter choice will result in better receptivity and learning, but lower status, since segregated instruction for a disadvantaged group will be assumed to be inferior.

The Clientele of Educational Programming for Older Persons

A fourth issue facing the field is the determination of the primary audience toward which education of older people will be directed. While older learners are different from younger learners, as noted in the previous section, they may be even more different from one another; several subgroups of older adults have, in fact, been identified. In light of this, a fundamental question presents itself: If educational programs are to be a significant force in improving the quality of life, should we concentrate our greater efforts on those subgroups that are most needy or on those which are more easily reached? Three areas in which subgroup differences are meaningful and bring up concerns for adult educators are: living arrangements, age, and educational level.

1. Should education serve isolated individuals or groups of older per-

sons? While high concentrations of older adults are found in certain areas of the country, older persons, in fact, live in every kind of setting: urban, suburban, rural; with families, in specialized housing projects, alone. Presently, educational programs best serve older adults who live in areas or settings with a high proportion of this age group. Less well served are the rural, homebound, or isolated elderly for whom the problems of survival and socialization, which might be addressed through education, are major. Reaching this group of persons remains a difficult problem. High-technology educational approaches (interactive TV, telephone instruction) do little to alleviate social isolation, but group activities present obvious transportation and mobility problems.

2. Should education serve the young-old or the old-old? Another important difference among older persons is the age group to which they belong. It has become clear that the so-called "young-old" age group (fifty-five to seventy) is quite different from the "old-old" group (seventy and over). Physical change and decline after the age of seventy dramatically influences the learning behavior of many persons. They typically become disadvantaged learners. Like those isolated by virtue of their living arrangements, the old-old are underserved by educational programs, in part because of inadequate efforts to reach and teach them.

3. Should education serve the sophisticated or inexperienced learner? A third important difference for educators is the educational level of older adults. Although generally lower relative to younger adults, the educational level of older persons varies widely. Those with more educational experience and more recent experience are often "savvy" learners, learners who need little encouragement to participate in educational programs and for whom nearly any method of teaching will work. Those with lower levels of formal education, "non-savvy" learners, are far less likely to participate in continuing education and may need more guidance when they do participate.

All of these subgroup differences may be summarized in one word: diversity. The issue concerns not only how to effectively manage the learning experience of a diverse group of persons, but whether and how to reach those subgroups that are presently underserved. Program planners need to decide whether this diverse population is best served through focusing efforts on those who easily and willingly participate in educational programs or through a more differentiated and complex response which has yet to be delineated.

Educational Providers for Older Persons

A fifth issue deals with the providers of instruction for older people. To date there has been a great array of providers at both the institutional level and the individual level. Several questions emerge from this situation:

1. What institutions, agencies, or organizations should coordinate educational activities or advocate the creation of additional programs? In a background paper on educational programs for older Americans, Howard McClusky (1971) noted the need to designate who should take primary responsibility for coordinating, initiating, and conducting educational programming for older persons? Should the responsibility lie principally with the educational system or with agencies that serve the aged? As McClusky points out, this is not an either/or issue. Indeed, older adults may be best served by the diversity of educational opportunities that arises when different types of agencies and institutions are involved in providing education for older persons. The question that remains, however, is who will be responsible to advocate for opportunities, to see to it that development of programs is advanced? Within the educational system, efforts to develop programs for older adults face competition from programs for children, youth, and young adults. On the other hand, within the network of aging services, education faces competition from the array of other social and health services provided and does not presently enjoy a high ranking in terms of financial support or focus of efforts. For educators, this issue has most meaning as we look for long-range guidance and support in planning and developing comprehensive educational programs for older adults.

2. Who should be the individual instructors of older persons and how should they be prepared? Concerning the first half of this question — who should instructors be — it is likely that diversity, as in types of institutional providers, is desirable. In fact, there has been research to show that older adults both enjoy and learn from instructors of all ages (Rindskopf, 1974). The use of older adults themselves as peer instructors, however, can be particularly effective. Regardless of their level of formal education, they are, at the very least, valuable resources in preserving our multiethnic national heritage. Depending on their own personal histories, their years of experience may well equip them to teach certain subjects better than the designated instructor. Furthermore, educators will raise the self-esteem and, subsequently, participation levels of older learners when they treat them as partners in the learning experience by making greater use of them as instructors. The issue for adult educators is deciding how to do this effectively. How can instructors make good use of the resources that older learners represent without abdicating their own responsibility for guiding the learning experience?

The second half of the question — how should instructors be prepared — is related. If instructors themselves continue to be a diverse group of people, it is likely that the degree to which they are prepared for teaching older adults will vary widely. Earlier in this chapter, it was noted that while laboratory studies have suggested useful guides for instructors of older adults, the many variations that exist within this population group as well as in the setting or content require a flexible teaching approach. Yet few persons who teach adults are familiar with basic knowledge about older persons, and fewer still with special techniques or procedures for teaching them. It would appear wise to prepare, through specialized educational programs or workshops, all persons who wish to instruct older learners, including older adults themselves. It is difficult to justify this as anything more than a useful suggestion, however, until there is more uniformity of preparation for all educators of adults. The issue is a broad one but not without special significance for the educators of older persons.

The provider issue, then, is actually two-pronged. When considering institutional, agency, or organizational providers the issue is one of deciding who should take the advocacy role in coordinating and initiating educational programs for older adults. When considering the individual provider the issue itself is a twofold one: Educators need to decide how best to use older adults themselves as instructors, and planners need to decide what level of preparedness for teaching older persons is minimally acceptable in their programs.

Financing Educational Programs

A sixth issue facing the education of older persons involves the generation of financial resources to support the planning and operation of these programs. In the past, the federal government has invested some resources in these activities, foundations have contributed to individual projects on an occasional basis, various educational providers have absorbed some of the costs, and the participants have typically paid a small fee. However, much of the real costs are covered by volunteer workers who subsidize the programs through their substantial contributions of time and effort. The issue of volunteerism has posed these questions:

1. Should voluntary staff operate educational programs for older people? In the long run, reliance on volunteerism is not a desirable strategy. Persons tire of contributing, older individuals experience illnesses, and administrators are unwilling to devote the necessary time to cultivate and support the volunteers. Consequently, real funds are needed to pay the staff and purchase the materials to successfully carry out the program.

At the same time, there is a danger in assuming that the use of paid instructors is without problems. Frequently, such instructors are paid at a low level, for a part-time commitment. Such arrangements often presume a certain level of volunteer effort and enthusiasm which may or may not exist. Special efforts must be made to ensure that part-time paid staff are provided opportunities for in-service education, for involvement in planning and development of programs offered, and in other ways to promote feelings of self-worth and a sense of being tied in with the organization.

2. What should be the primary sources of funding? Funding for programs could come from several sources: state government, the federal government, the sponsoring organization or agency, or foundations. In reality, none of these potential funders has the resources or the desire to support these activities. The future is likely to continue to see some combination of funding sources depending upon the purpose of the specific program. Those that provide coping or preventive services to older people who are in jeopardy are likely to receive some government funding, but others will undoubtedly have to fend for themselves. This is likely to mean that recreational, degree, social, and general instruction will be paid for by the older persons themselves.

The Shifting Sands of Knowledge

Perhaps one of the most important challenges for educators of older persons is the need to respond to changing issues and questions. The cookbook approach to solving problems is less appropriate today than it has ever been. Large social changes will have an impact on such institutions as the family, education, and the church, as well as influence the ability of the nation to ensure the health, financial security, and general welfare of all its citizens. What is known today about the needs of older persons in their social environment may well be inaccurate or superseded by more sophisticated information before the new decade is over.

The tremendous expansion of knowledge is likely to continue, at an even faster pace. Although technological advances are the most visible, advances in many other fields, including education and gerontology, are also being made. Greater sophistication in areas of present knowledge will be as important as new areas of investigation. For example, even over the last ten years the literature on aging has seen a shift from generalizations such as "intelligence declines with age" to "intelligence does not decline with age and, in fact, may even increase as we get older" to "intelligence is composed of many aspects, some of which appear to decline with age, others which improve, depending to a large extent on the individual, yet there may be a fairly universal decline in intellecual ability after the age of seventy." Such knowledge, revealing progressively more complex understandings of human development and learning, enables educators to develop more appropriate methods and content and to respond more meaningfully to the issues confronting older persons.

The aged cohort itself will undergo great changes in the future. The educational level of older persons will continue to rise, creating a greater demand for continuing education and, probably, a demand for more diverse offerings. Techniques and methods now thought more effective with older persons may no longer be recommended in twenty years as more people become classroom-wise and independent learning projects increase. The unique his-

84

torical period of time which future generations of old persons experience will shape their values, expectations, and activities in ways difficult to predict.

In conclusion, it is clear that learning to learn will be as important for continuing educators as it is for older adults. The issues of purpose, content, methods, clientele, providers, financing, and knowledge will require the continuing search for better ways of conceptualizing and providing educational experiences. The task will not be easy, but it is a task that should be undertaken as an affirmative enterprise, one which can be successfully completed and which will result in a better life for our older clients and a meaningful role for ourselves.

References

Aslanian, C. B., and Brickell, H. M. *Americans in Transition: Life Changes as Reasons for Adult Learning.* New York: College Entrance Examination Board. 1980.

Cross, K. P. *Adults as Learners: Increasing Participation and Facilitating Learning.* San Fran cisco: Jossey-Bass, 1981.

McClusky, H. Y. *Education: Background and Issues.* Washington, D.C.: White House Conference on Aging, 1971.

Palmore, E. "The Future Status of the Aged." *The Gerontologist,* 1976, *16,* 297-302.

Rinkskopf, K. "Instructor Age and the Older Learner." *The Gerontologist,* 1974, *14,* 479-482.

David A. Peterson is director of the Leonard Davis School of Gerontology at the University of Southern California. His professional interests are in the design of educational programs for older people and the conduct of gerontology instruction.

Rosemary A. Orgren recently received a Ph.D. in education from the University of Missouri–Columbia. She is a program planner at the Andrus Gerontology Center, University of Southern California.

Following an overview of the fledgling field of continuing education for older adults, several challenges and recommendations to practitioners are offered.

Reflections on Programs for Older Adults

Morris A. Okun

This chapter has two purposes: (1) to summarize the contents of the sourcebook and to integrate them with related literature; and (2) to reflect on the current scene in continuing education for older adults. The chapter is organized into six major sections that address the context of older adult education, age and cohort differences in participation, scope of programming, implications of psychological theorizing and research, the challenges faced by older adult education, and recommendations to programmers.

The Context of Older Adult Education

Gerontology is the scientific study of the process of aging and of older people (Atchley, 1977). There is a trade-off in differentiating older persons from others. On the one hand, it helps to focus on the unique aspects of late life. On the other hand, it promotes a view of older people as having little in common with younger people. Yet, we know that there is continuity in the psychological functioning of adults as they age (Neugarten, 1964). Describing older adults collectively is not easy as the task is complicated by their diversity and by social change which alters the characteristics of subsequent cohorts.

M. Okun (Ed.). *New Directions for Continuing Education: Programs for Older Adults*, no. 14. San Francisco: Jossey-Bass, June 1982.

As mentioned in the Editor's Notes, older adults, in the context of this sourcebook, include individuals at or beyond the age of fifty-five. Obviously, specifying a particular age as marking the onset of a new age status should be done only to provide a crude guideline. Neugarten (1975) has advanced the notion of two distinct groups of old people — the "young-old" (fifty-five to seventy) and the "old-old" (seventy one and older). This distinction should have some utility for continuing educators as the young-old have a higher participation rate in educational programs than the "old-old" (Heisel, Darkenwald, and Anderson, 1981).

Cross (1981) attributes the tremendous growth of lifelong education to three pervasive factors: demographic shifts, social change and technological change. The percentage of the U.S. population sixty-five and over rose steadily, but slowly, from 1950 to 1980. By 1990, the sixty-five years and older age group will probably comprise 12 percent of the U.S. population (Cross, 1981). Intergenerational differences and social-historical shifts have produced increased (1) leisure time, (2) variability in life styles, (3) educational attainment among cohorts of older adults, and (4) options for women (Birren and Woodruff, 1973; Schaie and Willis, 1978). The knowledge explosion has created serious problems in terms of professional obsolescence and job obsolescence which impact on the older worker (Dubin, 1972). Lastly, we may be seeing a shift, although hard to gauge, in the public's view of lifelong education. As Waskel points out in Chapter 3, the 1971 White House Conference on Aging proclaimed the basic right of older persons to educational opportunities. The Lifelong Learning Act of 1976 declares, in part, that opportunities for lifelong learning should be equivalent across all age groups.

Age and Cohort Differences in Participation

Age trends in participation in educational programs are based on cross-sectional analyses in which age of respondent is confounded with cohort membership (see Chapters 1 and 2). Thus, we do not have data on *changes in individuals'* participation over time. Keeping this qualifier in mind, it is important to examine *estimated* trends in participation by age *and* cohort.

The rate of participation appears to fall off sharply by age fifty-five (see Chapter 3; Graney, 1980). Spencer (1980) estimates that only 3 percent of the population over sixty years old participates in formal educational activities. The cohort trend, however, appears to be one of increased participation in the later years. The rate of participation by the fifty-five and over group climbed by 55 percent between 1969 and 1975, while the population of the fifty-five and over group increased by only 11.5 percent during the same period (Darkenwald and Merrian, 1982). Because subsequent cohorts will have higher educational attainment, be healthier, and so on, it is predicted that this trend of increased participation by the fifty-five and over group will continue in the immediate future (see Chapter 3; Drotter, 1981). It is also reasonable to predict a *lessening of the decline in participation by individuals during adulthood.*

Correlates of Participation Among Older Adults

Older participants relative to their younger counterparts are (1) less likely to use educational institutions and more likely to use unconventional locations; (2) less likely to be seeking credits; and (3) more likely to prefer alternative methods of instruction to classes and lectures (Arbeiter, 1976/1977). For current cohorts of older adults, the following factors appear to be correlated with participation: educational attainment, participation in community organizations, time spent reading, income, self-perceived health, being white and female (Heisel, Darkenwald, and Anderson, 1981; D. A. Peterson, 1981). It should be noted that the magnitude of the correlations reported are sometimes quite low (see Graney, 1980), indicating that many of the important predictors are unspecified in current research.

Presently, older cohorts generally have less formal education than younger cohorts and presumably need more education to catch up with their younger counterparts. Instead, they are less likely to participate, which serves only to widen the gap between the young and the older age groups. Within the older age group, the same phenonemon occurs with the "have nots" participating less than the "haves." Thus, we may be facing a situation where, paradoxically, older adults who need it the most are least likely to participate in educational programs.

Scope of Programs

In this section, older adult programs are reviewed with respect to settings, goals and objectives, motives of participation, and barriers.

Settings. Community-based organizations are the favorite location for older adult programs (Heisel, Darkenwald, and Anderson, 1981). Thorson (1978) states that churches appear to be the largest provider. Public schools and postsecondary educational institutions are predicted to become increasingly involved as centers for older adult education (McClusky, 1973). Clearly, in considering programs for current cohorts of older adults, it is necessary to develop strategies for reaching out to them instead of simply trying to pull them in (see Chapters 4–6).

Goals and Objectives. In reading program goal statements in this sourcebook, it appears that one common goal is related to successful aging (see Chapters 4–6). Successful aging can be defined as reaching late life and being in good health and happy (Palmore, 1979). Another common goal concerns empowering older people to control their own destinies (see Chapters 4–6; Moody, 1978). By empowering older people, they will be more effective in meeting their own needs (see Chapter 6) which, in turn, should lead them to age more successfully. Although inspection of program objectives reveals great diversity, the two goals mentioned above usually can be identified vis-a-vis specific objectives. For example, the empowering goal is operationalized in the Shepherd's center objective of "advocating the right of older people to a fair share of society's goods and to assist them in gaining access to services they need" (see Chapter 4). The successful aging goal is operationalized in an objective of the Creative Living Program of the Salinas Adult School: "to help students improve the quality of life in areas concerning their mental well being as well as their physical health" (Chapter 5).

Motives of Participants. A wide (and somewhat bewildering) array of approaches have been used to classify the motives of older adults for participating in programs. One approach has been to classify the education needs of older adults into categories such as coping, influence, expressive, contributive, and transcendence (see Chapter 3). Currently, the expressive need appears to be the one being met best of all. Should efforts be made to deal with the other motives in a more evenly distributed way (see Chapter 3; Hiemstra, 1976a; Moody, 1978)?

A second approach has focused on developmental tasks (Havighurst, 1972). Developmental tasks are physiological, psychological, and social demands a person must satisfy to be judged by others and by himself or herself as successful. Developmental tasks are linked to particular periods of adult life. Developmental tasks associated with late adulthood (approximately sixty-five and older) include adjusting to retirement, death of a spouse, and declining health and strength (Chickering and Havighurst, 1981). To be effective, programs should be aimed at those in late adult transition (approximately fifty-seven to sixty-five). In this way, individuals can be prepared to cope more effectively with the challenges posed by developmental tasks.

A third approach has focused on the motivational orientations of older adult participants. Motivational orientations refer to the primary reasons why adults participate in noncompulsory education (Houle, 1961). Boshier and Riddell (1978) found that older adults' (mean age = sixty-nine years) decision to participate was most strongly influenced by cognitive interest and social contact, whereas escape or stimulation and social welfare had little influence. The motivational orientations approach seems to have considerable utility for practitioners working with older people.

The final approach is a functional one in the sense that inferences are made about motives by examining the types of courses in which older adults actually enroll. Consistent with the motivational orientation research, personal interest seems to be the primary reason for participation (see Chapter 3;

Heisel, Darkenwald, and Anderson, 1981). However, older adults' subject area interests are quite varied (Hendrickson and Barnes, 1967).

Barriers. Barriers to participation can be classified under three headings: situational, institutional, and dispositional (Chapter 3; Cross, 1981). Situational barriers frequently mentioned by older adults include not enough time, poor vision, and cost. Institutional barriers often cited by older adults include the age-graded and depersonalized nature of educational institutions as well as lack of information. Compared to younger groups, those in the fifty-five and older group are more likely to mention lack of interest in education, poor health, and being too old to learn as common dispositional obstacles. In evaluating the research literature, it is important to note that questionnaires and interviews may produce socially desirable and superficial responses (Cross, 1981; Goodrow, 1975; Graney, 1980). The findings do seem to provide empirical support for the frequently made contention that older adults' attitudes toward themselves reflect society's attitude toward them (Kimmel, 1974).

Implications of Psychological Theorizing and Research

Theoretical analyses have called attention to the multivariate nature of life span development (Chapter 1; Schaie and Willis, 1978). Educators need to consider the independent and joint influence of intergenerational (cohort-related), ontogenetic (age-related), and sociocultural (period-related) factors. The implications of these factors for older adult programming are illustrated below. In terms of cohort-related differences, younger cohorts have more schooling than older cohorts and the best predictor of participation in continuing education is level of formal educational attainment (Arbeiter, 1976/1977). Thus, participation rates for older adults should rise in the future.

With regard to age-related changes, older adults are in, or about to enter, a life phase referred to as *life review, finishing up*. Associated with this phase is the psychic task of accepting what has transpired in life as having worth and meaning (Weathersby and Tarule, 1980). Finding creative ways to facilitate the synthesis of life experience into an integrated life structure is a vitally important function for older adult education (Chapter 1; Moody, 1978).

In terms of period-related effects, we can look at the implications of our currently high unemployment and inflation rates. During a period of job shortage, older people are pushed out of the job market and prevented from reentering (Best and Stern, 1976). However, if inflation is high, older adults are increasingly likely to seek additional income. Consequently, older adults may use educational programs as vehicles for updating their skills or for recareering (see Chapter 3, this volume; Boren, McCally, and Goldberg, 1979). From these examples, we see that knowledge of age-graded, socio-historical, and intergenerational factors can aid programmers in their efforts to alleviate, maintain, prepare, and enrich the lives of older adults (Chapter 1; Birren and Woodruff, 1973).

Life span developmental models are beginning to emphasize that older adults continue to develop, that they maintain their capability to learn, and that there is considerable plasticity in their cognitive functioning (see Chapter 1, this volume). In considering intervention effects, we should note that, despite good intentions, programs do not automatically have uniformly positive benefits on all participants. The programmer must distinguish between his or her view and the client's view on desired changes, realize that intervention can turn into invasion, and take some responsibility for unintended, undesirable outcomes (Hultsch, 1974).

Implications from Psychological Research. Hulicka and Gounard (Chapter 2) conclude that age differences in learning and memory performance "tend to be rather small up to the age range of sixty to seventy . . . mean differences between groups tend to be very small in comparison to the variability within age groups." In other words, age per se accounts for little of the variation in learning and memory performance.

As Hulicka and Gounard note, there are clusters of noncognitive factors affecting the learning process. These factors—motivational (anxiety), physiological (sensory acuity), experiential (type of education), and situational (classroom climate)—are important variables for instructors to consider (Bolton, 1978; Verner and Davidson, 1971; Woodruff and Walsh, 1975). However, over and above the noncognitive factors, older adults do not appear to be as efficient information processors as their younger counterparts. In looking for the loci of age differences in memory, psychologists have postulated attentional (Schaie and Willis, 1978), encoding (Botwinick, 1978), and retrieval (Hartley, Harker, and Walsh, 1980) deficits. Clearly, some of these factors are under the control of instructors. For example, the instructional parameters of pacing, information input channels, meaningfulness and organization of the material, and learning activities can all be arranged to enhance the effectiveness of the instructional process (Gounard and Hulicka, 1977).

Interestingly, several of the suggestions offered by Price (Chapter 5) dovetail with the recommendations emanating from the laboratory. Price suggests creating nonschool-like environments where people feel at ease, using peers as models, building more difficult tasks on easier ones, integrating content with life experience, employing discovery types of activities, and facilitating the learning process.

Current theorizing in cognitive psychology suggests two hypotheses for age-related deficits (Craik and Simon, 1980). The processing deficit hypothesis states that young adults spontaneously employ deeper levels of processing than older adults. In contrast, the production deficiency hypothesis states that the age deficit is due to older adults' failure to carry out operations which they are capable of implementing (see Chapter 1 for a similar hypothesis about activation). If the production hypothesis is valid, then it may be possible to enhance the recall of older adults by having them practice "deep processing" activities until their execution dissipates less "cognitive energy" (Craik and Simon, 1980, p. 107).

Future Directions for Research on Instruction. Hulicka and Gounard (Chapter 1) urge laboratory researchers to talk with practitioners to identify new problems. Their exhortation reflects the current imbalance between laboratory and field research on cognition and aging. While basic research on cognitive processes and aging should be maintained, there is a dearth of naturalistic studies of learning and memory in and out of the classroom (Hartley, Harker, and Walsh, 1980). Researchers should use ethnographic techniques (Wilson, 1977) to provide a thick, holistic description of the cognitive tasks older adults face within and outside of formal educational settings. Such research can then be linked with correlational and field and laboratory experimental studies.

Challenges to Practitioners

Several issues enumerated by Peterson and Orgren (Chapter 8) are briefly elaborated on in this section. First, there is the challenge to providers to be "beacons as opposed to mirrors" of society. That educational opportunities in this country remain highly age-graded indicates that providers are operating more on the mirror than on the beacon principle (Ecklund, 1969). Darkenwald and Merriam (1982) note that much of adult education is irrelevant to the concerns of many older people. From the perspective of social transformation, older adults represent an appropriate group to "liberate" as they are devalued by our society and have a negative self-image regarding learning ability (Moody, 1978). Moody suggests that many of the principles espoused and used by Friere (1970) are germane to raising the critical consciousness of older adults.

A second challenge, related to the first one, is to increase the participation of older adults, in general, and of lower status older adults, in particular. Waskel (Chapter 3) argues for a systematic set of priorities for older adult education. Clearly, values come into play in establishing priorities as does their feasibility. Is it surprising that a middle-class group of professionals should cater to middle-class learners and to those older adults who are more formally educated? Eklund (1969) estimates that 20 percent of all people over sixty-five are functional illiterates. The triple jeopardy of lower status, being older, and not being functionally literate creates tremendous obstacles with regard to successful aging (Drotter, 1981). Will this challenge become a major priority? Finally, it is likely that future cohorts of older adults will be even more diverse, given the accelerating rate of social change (Chapter 1; Thorson, 1978). How do we meet the challenge of dealing with heterogeneous learners?

The third challenge is to decide how programs will be funded. As Maves (Chapter 4) comments, funding is a perpetual problem. Price (Chapter 5) has as an objective the delivery of cost effective programs. Do educational programs have to break even or show a profit to be continued? How do we assess the benefit side of the cost-benefit equation? Currently, evaluation is typically limited to head counts and perceived satisfaction with the program (Maves, Chapter 4; D. A. Peterson, 1980). Clearly, program evaluations will be necessary both to improve programs and for advocacy purposes (see Chapter 3).

The fourth challenge concerns who will be the providers. Demko (Chapter 6) warns us of the instant gerontology phenomenon. As postsecondary educational institutions seek new clientele, some may decide to get on the bandwagon without much thought to programming and providers (D. A. Peterson, 1981).

There are also turf-related issues. Will providers work together to optimize opportunities for older adult learners or will they compete with each other (Chapter 7)? The challenge may be to find ways to integrate education with community service (Chapter 3; Heisel, Darkenwald, and Anderson, 1981).

In a somewhat different vein, to what extent should older adults run their own programs? Volunteers already play a vital role in many programs (Chapters 4 and 5). Should programs be headed up by professionally trained peers? Programs by and for older adults might be more forceful in the advocacy arena.

The last challenge pertains to the relationship between self-directed learning (see Chapter 3) and education. Unfortunately, we have been sloppy in our usage of the terms lifelong learning and lifelong education (see Farmer, 1974). Consequently, there has been a tendency to equate the lack of participation in formal educational activities with lack of learning. R. E. Peterson (1981) reminds us that everyone learns unintentionally by living. He also points out that intentional, independent (self-planned and self-initiated) learning occurs more frequently than participation in formal education. Interestingly, the association between age and participation in formal education appears to be much greater than the association between age and participation in self-directed learning efforts (Arbeiter, 1976/1977; Hiemstra, 1976b; Penland, 1979). The challenge then is to find a useful role for educational programs in facilitating self-directed learning of older adults. In doing this, care must be taken not to institutionalize lifelong schooling (Gueulette, 1981) and not to make self-directed learners dependent on the providers (Hiemstra, 1976b).

Recommendations to Practitioners

The list of recommendations is divided into facilitating participation and facilitating learning. The points enumerated in both sections are based on the other sourcebook chapters and the writings of Cross (1981), Goodrow (1975), Miller (1967), Okun (1977), and Spencer (1980).

Facilitating Participation

1. Develop a coordinated network of formal and nonformal educational providers.
2. Link the network to many community agencies (for example, Area Agency on Aging) and local businesses and financial institutions.
3. Develop a synchronized delivery system among providers. Have a guide to educational opportunities available and get it out to your target group.
4. "Position" to empower other providers as well as yourself.
5. Use a variety of recruiting methods, including mass media, workshops, and posters and brochures placed in high visibility locations (for example, banks).
6. The "grapevine" is the most critical form of marketing; learner satisfaction must be high.
7. Use learners and volunteers as recruiters. Target your recruitment efforts on community gatekeepers.
8. The recruitment message should be positive, contain specific information, and reflect knowledge of the community. For example, if the local populace contains many activity-oriented learners, posters should reflect images of older adults engaged in lively discussion in a relaxed and comfortable environment.
9. Bring the program to the people. Outreach efforts should take advantage of locales naturally frequented by older adults (such as churches, senior centers, and parks, as well as other convenient sites such as public schools.) Where travel is unavoidable, consider mobile units, school buses, car pooling, and television-based courses.
10. Keep fees minimal; charge something.
11. Consider local conditions in scheduling (for example, time of day, length of sessions, frequency of meetings per week, and length of instructional units).
12. Build positive attitudes toward education by demonstrating products through arts and crafts fairs, publishing an anthology of po-

etry, profiling successful individuals, and obtaining local coverage by media. Have open houses.

13. Create a sense of ownership among participants. Become a community resource. Use the community as an advocacy group.

Facilitating Learning

1. Create educational opportunities for anxious learners which entail low levels of risk and threat.
2. Build on success experiences; integrate unfamiliar with familiar material.
3. Emphasize the informal as opposed to the formal aspects of the educational experience.
4. Emphasize self-directed and intrinsically motivating activities.
5. Use participatory instructional strategies which emphasize peers as resources.
6. Take advantage of teachable moments engendered by life transitions and developmental tasks.
7. Integrate life experience with the learning process.
8. Meet the goals of the learners. For example, "cognitive interest" learners should have ample opportunities to deal seriously with topics, while "social contact" learners should have ample opportunities to interact with others.
9. Conceptualize and assess how instructional activities relate to objectives and goals.
10. Emphasize informational feedback rather than judgmental evaluation.
11. Remove physiological barriers.
12. When teaching new information or skills, use self-pacing, avoid introducing irrelevant information, encourage learners to use encoding and retrieval strategies, and promote learning to learn.
13. Respect diversity among learners and try to individualize at least some aspects of the instructional process.

Continuing education for older adults appears to be a growing area of programming. The overview of concepts, research findings, and practice in this sourcebook provides some practical suggestions and ideas for practitioners who want to initiate or expand their service to the "young-old" and the "old-old." As Price (Chapter 5) has indicated, programmers will have to "go with the flow" to cope successfully with changing older adults in a changing world (Riegel, 1979). We need imaginative educators who, as Cross (1981, p. 149) states, " . . . can formulate new programs, perhaps undreamed of by potential learners, that strike people as a better way to do things."

References

Atchley, R. C. *The Social Forces in Later Life* (2nd ed.) Belmont, Calif.: Wadsworth, 1977.

Arbeiter, S. "Profile of the Adult Learner." *The College Board Review,* 1976/1977, *102,* 20–26.

Best, F., and Stern, B. *Lifetime Distribution of Education, Work, and Leisure.* Washington, D.C.: Institute for Educational Leadership, Postsecondary Convening Authority, 1976.

Birren, J. E., and Woodruff, D. "Human Development Over the Life Span Through Education." In P. B. Baltes and K. W. Schaie (Eds.), *Life Span Development Psychology: Personality and Socialization.* New York: Academic Press, 1973.

Bolton, E. B. "Cognitive and Noncognitive Factors That Affect Learning in Older Adults and Their Implications for Instruction." *Educational Gerontology,* 1978, *3,* 331–344.

Boren, N., McCally, M., and Goldberg, R. "A Career Transition Program for Older Persons." *Educational Gerontology,* 1979, *4,* 1–18.

Boshier, R., and Riddell, G. "Education Participating Scale Factor Structure for Older Adults." *Adult Education,* 1978, *28,* 165–175.

Botwinick, J. *Aging and Behavior: A Comprehensive Integration of Research Findings.* (2nd ed.) New York: Springer, 1978.

Chickering, A. W., and Havighurst, R. J. "The Life Cycle." In A. W. Chickering and Associates (Eds.), *The Modern American College.* San Francisco: Jossey-Bass, 1981.

Craik, F. I. M., and Simon, E. "Age Differences in Human Memory: The Role of Attention and Depth of Processing." In L. W. Poon, J. L. Fozard, L. S. Cermak, D. Arenberg, and L. W. Thompson (Eds.), *New Directions in Memory and Aging: Proceedings of the George Talland Memorial Conference.* Hillsdale, N.J.: Erlbaum, 1980.

Cross, K. P. *Adults as Learners.* San Francisco: Jossey-Bass, 1981.

Darkenwald, G. G., and Merriam, S. B. *Adult Education: Foundations of Practice.* New York: Harper & Row, 1982.

Drotter, M. W. "Education for the Elderly: Trends and Problems in the 1980s." *Educational Gerontology,* 1981, *7,* 105–110.

Dubin, S. S. "Obsolescence or Lifelong Education: A Choice for the Professional." *American Psychologist,* 1972, *27,* 486–498.

Ecklund, L. "Aging and the Field of Education." In J. W. Riley, Jr. and E. M. Johnson (Eds.), *Aging and Society.* New York: Russell Sage Foundation, 1969.

Farmer, J. A., Jr. "Impact of 'Lifelong Learning' on the Professionalization of Adult Education." *Journal of Research and Development in Education,* 1974, *7,* 57–67.

Friere, P. *Pedagogy of the Oppressed.* New York: Herder and Herder, 1970.

Goodrow, B. A. "Limiting Factors in Reducing Participation in Older Adult Learning Opportunities." *Gerontologist,* 1975, *15,* 418–422.

Gounard, B. R., and Hulicka, I. M. "Maximizing Learning Efficiency in Later Adulthood: A Cognitive Problem-Solving Approach." *Educational Gerontology,* 1977, *2,* 417–427.

Graney, M. J. "Participation in Education Among Older People." *Alternative Higher Education,* 1980, *5,* 71–86.

Gueulette, D. G. "Visions of Spectres." *Adult Education,* 1981, *31,* 37–43.

Hartley, J. T., Harker, J. V., and Walsh, P. A. "Contemporary Issues and New Directions in Adult Development of Learning and Memory." In L. W. Poon (Ed.), *Aging in the 1980s: Psychological Issues.* Washington, D.C.: American Psychological Association, 1980.

Havighurst, R. J. *Developmental Tasks and Education.* (3rd ed.) New York: McKay, 1972.

Heisel, M. A., Darkenwald, G. G., and Anderson, R. E. "Participation in Organized Educational Activities Among Adults Age Sixty and Over." *Educational Gerontology,* 1981, *6,* 227–240.

Hendrickson, A., and Barnes, R. F. "Educational Needs of Older People." *Adult Leadership,* 1967, *16,* 2–4.

Hiemstra, R. "Older Adult Learning: Instrumental and Expressive Categories." *Educational Gerontology,* 1976a, *1,* 227–236.

Hiemstra, R. "The Older Adult's Learning Projects." *Educational Gerontology,* 1976b, *1,* 331–341.

Houle, C. O. *The Design of Education.* Madison: University of Wisconsin Press, 1961.

Hultsch, D. F. "Why Are We Trying to Teach Adults?" In D. F. Hultsch and R. W. Bortner (Eds.), *Interventions in Learning: The Individual and Society.* University Park: The Pennsylvania State University, 1974.

Kimmel, D. C. *Adulthood and Aging.* New York: Wiley, 1974.

McClusky, H. Y. "Education and Aging." In A. Hendrickson (Ed.), *A Manual on Planning Educational Programs for Older Adults.* Tallahassee: Florida State University, 1973.

Miller, H. L. *Participation of Adults in Education: A Force-Field Analysis.* Boston: Center for the Study of Liberal Education for Adults, Boston University, 1967.

Moody, H. R. "Education and the Life Cycle: A Philosophy of Aging." In R. H. Sherron and D. B. Lumsden (Eds.), *Introduction to Educational Gerontology.* New York: Hemisphere, 1978.

Neugarten, B. L., and Associates. *Personality in Middle and Late Life.* New York: Atherton, 1964.

Neugarten, B. L. "The Future and the Young-Old." *Gerontologist,* 1975, *15,* 4–9 (supplement).

Okun, M. A. "Implications of Geropsychological Research for the Instruction of Older Adults." *Adult Education,* 1977, *25,* 139–155.

Palmore, E. "Predictors of Successful Aging." *Gerontologist,* 1979, *19,* 427–431.

Penland, P. "Self-Initiated Learning." *Adult Education,* 1979, *29,* 170–179.

Peterson, D. A. "Who Are the Educational Gerontologists?" *Educational Gerontology,* 1980, *5,* 65–77.

Peterson, D. A. "Participation in Education by Older People." *Educational Gerontology,* 1981, *7,* 245, 256.

Peterson, R. E. "Opportunities for Adult Learners." In A. W. Chickering and Associates. *The Modern American College.* San Francisco: Jossey-Bass, 1981.

Riegel, K. F. *Foundations of Dialectical Psychology.* New York: Academic Press, 1979.

Schaie, K. W., and Willis, S. L. "Life Span Development: Implications for Education." In L. S. Shulman (Ed.), *Review of Research in Education.* Itasca, Ill.: Peacock, 1978.

Spencer, B. "Overcoming the Age Bias of Continuing Education." In G. Darkenwald and G. Larson (Eds.), *New Directions for Continuing Education: Reaching Hard-to-Reach Adults,* no. 8. San Francisco: Jossey-Bass, 1980.

Thorson, J. A. "Future Trends in Education for Older Adults." In R. H. Sherron and D. B. Lumsden (Eds.), *Introduction to Educational Gerontology.* New York: Hemisphere, 1978.

Verner, C., and Davison, C. V. *Physiological Factors in Adult Learning and Instruction.* Tallahassee: Florida State University, 1971.

Weathersby, R. P., and Tarule, J. M. *Adult Development: Implications for Higher Education.* Washington, D.C.: American Association for Higher Education, 1980.

Wilson, S. "The Use of Ethnographic Techniques in Educational Research." *Review of Educational Research,* 1977, *40,* 245–265.

Woodruff, D. S., and Walsh, D. A. "Research in Adult Learning: The Individual." *Gerontologist,* 1975, *15,* 424–430.

Morris A. Okun is an associate professor in the Department of Higher and Adult Education, Arizona State University. His current research and teaching focus on educational and psychological gerontology.

Index

Retirement planning seminars, 39, 59–60
Riddell, G., 88, 95
Riegel, K. F., 94, 96
Riley, J. W., 5, 10, 26, 34, 95
Rinkskopf, K., 81, 84
Rivera, R. J., 27, 34
Robertson, B. A., 19, 24
Robertson-Tchabo, E. A., 13, 23
Rosemary, A. O., 75–84
Rural populations, 80; programs for, 47
Rust, L. D., 17, 23

S

Salinas Adult School, 46, 48. *See also* Creative Living Program
Salinas Union High School District, 45, 52
Schaie, K. W., 6–8, 10, 23, 86, 89–90, 96
Schonfeld, D., 19, 24
Self-pacing, and cognitive process, 19, 30–31
Senior Center Humanities Program, Dane County, Wis., 70–71
Senior centers, 70
Senior Educational Activity Centers (SEAC), Salinas, Ca., 49
Shanas, E., 10
Shearon, R. W., 28, 33
Shepherd's Center: activities of, 40–41; Board of Directors of, 41; founding of, 35–37; programs of, 37–41; recommendations drawn from, 43–44; reflections on, 42–43; staffing and administration of, 41–42; Training Service, 36
Sherron, R. H., 33, 96
Shulman, L. S., 96
Simon, E., 90–91, 95
Social change orientation, 9, 61, 76–77, 87–88
Speech therapy course, 49
Spencer, B., 86, 93, 96
St. Luke's Methodist Church, Oklahoma City, 37
Staff, 41–42, 51–52. *See also* Administration; Instructors
Stern, B., 89, 95

Stimulus/response output, and learning, 15–18
Stock, W. A., 18, 24
Survey research, 64

T

Tarule, J. M., 89, 96
Technology issues, 30, 80
Templin, R. G., 33
Thompson, L. W., 95
Thorndike, E. L., 3, 10
Thorson, J. A., 87, 92, 96
Tough, A., 31, 33–34
Transcendence needs, 28
Trehub, S. E., 23
Tutoring program, 51

U

U.S. Bureau of the Census, 26, 34

V

Verner, G., 90, 96
Volunteer staff, 38, 51, 82, 92; training of, 41–43
"Volunteer to Live," 36

W

Walsh, P. A., 18, 23, 90–91, 95–96
Waskel, S., 25–34, 91
Wasserman, J. W., 27, 34
Weathersby, R. P., 89, 96
Welford, A. T., 16, 24
White House Conference on Aging, 25, 86
Wilkie, F., 17, 23
Williams, M. V., 16, 23
Willis, L. S., 3–11, 19, 24, 86, 89–90, 96
Wilson, S., 91, 96
Wisconsin Bureay of Aging, 69
Witte, K. L., 16, 24
Woodruff, D., 90, 95–96
Woods, A. M., 16, 23

Y

"Young-old" learner, 86